WHY AMERICA IS FREE

A History of the Founding
of the American Republic
1750-1800

Kenneth E. Hamburger, Ph.D.
Joseph R. Fischer, Ph.D.
Steven C. Gravlin, Lt.Col., USA

Published by the Mount Vernon Ladies' Association
for
The Society of the Cincinnati
2118 Massachusetts Avenue, NW
Washington, D.C. 20008

Tel: 202/785-2040   Fax: 202/785-0729

Published for
The Society of the Cincinnati
by
The Mount Vernon Ladies' Association
Mount Vernon, Virginia
© 1998 by The Mount Vernon Ladies' Association
All rights reserved. Published 1998.

Cover illustration: *Washington Before Yorktown*
by Rembrandt Peale, 1824-1825
The Corcoran Gallery of Art, Washington, D.C.

ISBN: 0-931917-29-8

WHY AMERICA IS FREE
A History of the Founding
of the American Republic
1750-1800

The Education Committee of The Society of the Cincinnati

Dave R. Palmer, Chairman	Eugene Jenkins	Minor Myers, Jr.
William W. Anderson, V	Warren M. Little, Ed. D.	William R. Raiford
Albert S. Britt, III	Kleber S. Masterson, Jr.	A. Preston Russell, M.D.
Frederick L. Graham	William M. Matthew	Lewis S. Sorley, III
George T. Harrison		W. Keats Sparrow, Ph.D.

Executive Editor	**Managing Editor**	**Senior Editor**
George T. Harrison	William T. Still	A. Preston Russell, M.D.

Associate Editors

Mrs. George Fenwick Jones, M.S.A.
Paul Pressly, Ph.D.
Dave R. Palmer, President, Walden University
Thad W. Tate, Ph.D.

Contributing Editors

William Abbot	John D. Kilbourne	Lawrence Murdoch, Jr.
William W. Anderson, V	Richard Krohn, Ph.D.	Minor Myers, Jr.
Professor Richard Beeman	George Varich Lauder	Ralph Maxwell Payne
Albert S. Britt, III	Mrs. Daniel Lesesne	Jeffrey Pendleton
Brian W. Brooke	Clifford Lewis, III	Michael C. Quinn
Charles Claghorn, III	Warren M. Little, Ed.D.	William R. Raiford
Ellen McCallister Clark	Mark F. Lloyd	James C. Rees
H. Bartholomew Cox	Kleber S. Masterson, Jr.	Lewis S. Sorley, III
Frederick L. Graham	William M. Matthew	W. Keats Sparrow, Ph.D.
Lewis S. Graham, Jr.	Reverend William McKeachie	E. Tillman Stirling, Esq.
William Hershey Greer	Philippus Miller, V	John C. Tuten, Jr.
Thomas Hardie	John Muhlenberg	Dorothy Twohig
Eugene Jenkins		Peter S. Wheeler, Esq.

THE SOCIETY OF THE CINCINNATI

The Society of the Cincinnati is an organization of descendants of commissioned officers who served in the regular (Continental) American Army or Navy and the French Army or Navy the Revolution. The oldest organization of its kind in the United States, it has been continuously active since its founding in 1783. The Society is a not-for-profit organization whose mission is to support educational, cultural, and literary activities that promote the ideals of liberty and constitutional government.

Pictured above: George Washington's Diamond Eagle pin, one of the most treasured objects in the Society of the Cincinnati collection.

Table of Contents

When the British invaded New York City, many patriots decided it would be better to burn important structures rather than allow them to fall into British hands. This was one of many sacrifices made to ultimately win the war.

Introduction

Freedom: The American Dream
The American Responsibility

The United States of America is a young country compared to many nations around the world. Though young, America has already given its citizens more freedom than any other nation in history. We are free to follow our personal paths to success, so long as we behave responsibly. From that freedom has grown great national wealth and strength.

How did freedom happen? How can we remain free? Answering these questions is a very important responsibility for all citizens of our country.

Our freedom did not happen by accident. It was difficult to achieve. Many Americans gave their lives earning and defending it. As citizens of a free country we are privileged, but liberty is a privilege that must be continually protected.

How can we preserve our freedom?

At one of the many naturalization ceremonies where new citizens pledge their allegiance to America, a spirit of patriotism fills the air.

We must do two things. First of all, we have to understand how valuable it is. How can we do that? – by understanding the terrible price our ancestors paid to gain it. Secondly, we must never forget the ideas our ancestors struggled to preserve. How do we do that? – by discovering how our country was born.

WHY STUDY HISTORY?

History is the record of what our ancestors did. It is the story of what they thought and how they tried to solve the problems they faced. By reading their stories we can learn about our own lives. We can learn from the mistakes and the successes of many lifetimes squeezed into a few pages. People are considered wise when they learn from experience. In our families, we respect the advice of our parents because they have lived through many more events than we have. They've seen more history. We can achieve more by learning from successes and failures of the past. Understanding our history is the best way to preserve our freedom.

THE AMERICAN DREAM

A nation which gives us lots of freedom naturally gives us lots of opportunities to be successful – to live out our dreams. And that's what the American experiment is all about. Experiment? Yes. This is a great experiment. It started as an entirely new form of government that had never been tried before. What was new about it? That's the key question. Here's the answer: democracy. In this country lots of people share power – the power to vote – the power to run for office – the power to speak their minds freely. Americans believe these are God-given rights, not privileges which can be revoked by a government.

Thanks to this concept, millions of people from around the world have flocked to America. All these people shared something in common: a belief that if they worked hard, they could make a better future for themselves and their families. That's what we call the "American Dream."

This American Dream can mean something different for each one of us. For some, it can mean becoming wealthy or having important or powerful jobs. For others, it might mean getting married and raising children. Perhaps some want to become a great doctor, teacher, minister, or lawyer, performer, engineer, manufacturer, inventor or football player. Probably many hope to follow in their father's or mother's footsteps. The point is that we all have a dream, and the United States of America is the place that promises each of us a chance to fulfill it.

THE AMERICAN RESPONSIBILITY

Although the American experiment gives us great opportunities to succeed, it also involves special responsibilities. We have to be more careful to prevent the mistakes that freedom allows us to make. For example, we have a right to freely speak our mind, but we cannot purposely lie about someone to embarrass them. How do we learn about our responsibilities? — by studying how we got here and by studying American history. We have a clear choice: either we learn from our history or we are doomed to repeat the mistakes of the past and lose our freedom.

What will happen if we lose our freedom? We may suffer the same fate of other countries in which people can't speak freely, meet freely, talk about ideas freely. In some countries, people are not permitted to decide what work they want to do, who they can marry, or when to have children. In such countries the government tells them what to do and when to do it. The choice is to obey or be punished. Our democracy — our right to help decide what our government does — is strengthened when Americans know their history.

Thomas Jefferson said "Eternal vigilance is the price of liberty." Liberty means freedom. Vigilance means to watch things closely. When we study our past we are watching closely. We understand why our ancestors cherished liberty and it becomes clear that we cannot take freedom for granted — it has been lost and regained again and again. And it all began with the founding fathers. Among the best things young citizens can do is to study the form of government our forefathers set up to preserve the freedom earned during the Revolutionary War.

That's what this book is all about — to help us understand our past — to remind us why we are free. That's freedom's special responsibility.

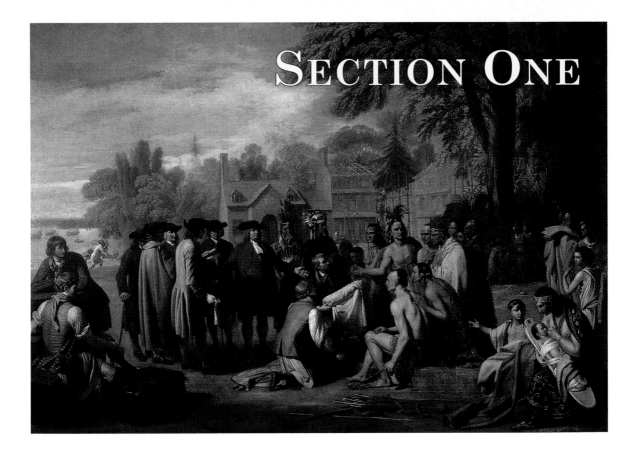

SECTION ONE

BEFORE THE REVOLUTION

Above, William Penn negotiates a treaty with the Indians in 1771-72. Painting by Benjamin West from the Pennsylvania Academy of Fine Arts. *At left, members of the Boy Scouts of America learn how to survey land at Mount Vernon. George Washington's first occupation was that of a surveyor of the western territories.*

Old Bruton Parish Church in Williamsburg, Virginia, was a central place of worship for colonists before, during and after the Revolutionary War. Painting by A. Wordsworth Thompson.

Chapter 1

A Colonial Breakfast

FEBRUARY 22, 1750

Jed woke up early. It was cold in his tiny attic loft, but the heavy homespun blankets that covered him felt warm. Below him he could hear his father stirring up the fire in the fireplace that heated his family's stone and log cabin. Like it or not, it was time to get up. Then he remembered – today was special. He sat up and pushed open the heavy shutters that covered the window by his bed.

Though the sun was not yet up, Jed could see an orange glow through the trees that stood near the cabin built by his father's own hands in the Virginia woods. He saw a small herd of deer disappear into the trees as the shutters' hinges squeaked.

"Jed, it's time to get up and do your chores," his father called softly from the room below. "Did you hear me, Jed?"

"Yes, Papa. I was already awake."

"And ... happy birthday, Jed."

It was Jedidiah Warwick's ninth birthday. Jed's family lived in Virginia on the peninsula between Williamsburg and Yorktown. Their cabin overlooked a wonderful source of fresh water, Skiffes Creek, which ran into the mighty James River a couple of miles away.

Jed held his breath as he threw back his quilt, jumped out of bed, scooped up his icy cold clothes, and climbed quickly down the narrow homemade ladder to the room below.

He wanted to finish dressing by the fire. Its flames were now crackling and popping around fresh logs. By the time he felt its warmth, his teeth were already chattering. Hastily he plunged his feet into his heavy knit wool stockings, then jerked up his wool pants. Next, he whipped off his nightshirt and pulled his linen shirt and then a leather vest over his head.

MORNING CHORES

Last of all, Jed slipped into the coarse wooden clogs his father had carved for him as a Christmas present and ran out to the barn to feed the animals. He was hungry, too, but the livestock always came first. The sooner he filled their stomachs, the sooner he could be filling his own.

He closed the bottom half of the barn door and cracked the top half open to let the faint light in. Jed took a deep breath. He loved the rich smell of the hay and the cattle. Once inside, he picked up a wooden pitchfork and scooped some hay into the hollowed-out log that served as a feed trough. Their

On special occasions, a formal dinner table included treats like the holiday pie at the center of the table, and boiled leg of lamb.

huge ox, Brownie, was already waiting for his breakfast, and Jed could feel the animal's warm breath on his arm as he filled the manger. Jed heard their cow, Sarah, groaning as she heaved herself up from the straw near the wall. Soon she was next to Brownie, munching the hay.

Tom Warwick arrived a moment later, carrying a wooden bucket. Taking down a small stool from a peg on the wall, he sat down next to Sarah and began milking her. Jed watched the warm milk squirting into the bucket for a moment, raising steam in the dawn chill. Since Sarah had given milk all

11

The kitchen at George Washington's home, Mount Vernon, is separate from the main house, to keep the hazard of fire away from the home. The smoke, heat and odors from a busy kitchen would also disturb the guests in the house.

summer and autumn, she was almost dry by winter. Then Jed went out into the small lean-to attached to the barn to let their four sheep and two goats out into the barnyard.

The barnyard was a small pasture area enclosed by a stone-and-rail fence. But since it was wintertime, and there was no green grass to eat, Jed carried two pitchforks of fresh hay out to the manger in the barnyard as well.

As the sun broke over the eastern horizon, with the first rays dazzling off the crystal frost on the ground, Jed and his father walked back to the house together.

Jed shivered, "Aren't you cold, Papa?"

"Yes, but it's only a few weeks until spring. It makes me warmer just to think about it." He tousled Jed's hair. "Besides, all you need is a little more work to heat you up," he grinned. "I want to make sure we're ready to plant our garden next month, so after school for the next few days, I want you to rake up all of last year's garden so it's clean. Then as soon as the weather breaks, we can plow it." Jed's father thought for a moment. "But you don't have to start today since it's your birthday."

Jed smiled back into his father's weather-beaten face. "Thank you, Papa. But I'll do a little this afternoon if I get home in time. Right now, what I really need is a good, hot breakfast." Tom Warwick laughed as they hurried back into the kitchen side of the warm cabin.

THE CABIN

The Warwick cabin was built directly on the ground with its posts buried in the earth. Interlocking logs made the walls of the two-room building. The two rooms were connected by a porch between them. One room was the living area where there was a large wooden bed with a cornshuck mattress for Jed's parents and a smaller bed where Jed's little sister slept. Above them was the small loft where Jed slept. A blackened fireplace was at one end of the room. The only other furniture in the room was a spinning wheel and a small loom for making cloth, a little table of rough-hewn split logs, and two cane-seat chairs.

The room on the other side of the porch was called the "kitchen side." The kitchen was smaller than the living room/bedroom, but its big cooking fireplace made the room very warm. Kitchens were separated from the main house in those days for two reasons:

1. In the summertime, when it was hot, cooking was still done on the big cooking fireplace, so the hot kitchen was set away from the rest of the house.

2. In case the kitchen side of the house caught on fire, the rest of the house might be saved.

BREAKFAST

Jed and his father entered the kitchen when they returned from the barn. Jed's mother, Mary Warwick, and his sister, Abigail, were already working on breakfast. Jed's mother had placed a single wooden platter on a table.

On the platter were four slabs of steaming cornbread smeared with bacon fat. Alongside the platter was a pottery bowl of dried apple slices. Jed's father set his bucket of milk on the small work table against the wall. Using a gourd dipper, his mother filled four pottery cups with milk. Then, she poured the rest of the fresh milk into a crock so she could skim the cream off later that day. Jed and his father sat on a log bench on one side of the table, and his mother and sister sat on the other side. As before every meal, they bowed their heads while Jed's father said grace.

"We humbly thank the Almighty for bringing us through another night and for providing so bountifully for our well-being. Bless us all, and bless Jed on his birthday, and bless good King George and those who govern under him. Amen."

Tom Warwick smiled as he watched his children eat. They both had healthy appetites. He reached for the apple slices to go along with the cornbread. "I'm going to try to finish the mill house by the end of next month. That way we can be ready to begin grinding our grain by spring. John Franklin says he'll have his team of oxen and a half-dozen slaves start to work as soon as they can.

"If all goes well, we should be running the only mill between Williamsburg and Yorktown by summer. Jed, you're going to have plenty to do when school's out." Jed smiled, happy that his father thought he was old enough to be of help in the new mill business. As the meal ended, as was the

Inside the kitchen, there was usually a huge fireplace and plenty of pots, bowls, and spits to cook for a large number of guests.

This barn was designed by George Washington to provide an inside location for the treading of wheat, which was beginning to take the place of tobacco as a cash crop in Tidewater Virginia in the 1750s and 1760s.

custom, grace was offered again.

As Jed walked to school at the nearby parish church, he imagined the wonderful adventures he and Abby would have fishing in their own mill pond when summertime came.

OPPORTUNITY

The Warwick family were called colonists in the America of 1750. Most colonists in Virginia were English citizens, since they or someone in their families before them had crossed the Atlantic Ocean to settle in the new land called America. They lived in new states, called colonies, that belonged to Britain.

Most Colonists had to get along on their own. They hunted and grew their own food. They built their own homes, barns, and fences. They could even make most of the household items they needed. Like other colonists, the Warwick family was very self-sufficient. They considered America a land of great opportunity, rich with natural resources and the freedom to use them. Jed's parents had come from England along with thousands of other new immigrants in the last decade. Most were poor and had little chance of changing their fortunes back home.

When Jed's father finished the new mill, the family would move up in class to the status of merchants and small farmers. Even though their standard of living was crude by today's standards, the Warwicks were

14

already living better than their parents had in England. Though life was hard and filled with chores from sun-up to sun-down, they were already comfortable and really had everything they needed.

THE GEOGRAPHY OF THE TIDEWATER

The Tidewater is that part of the mid-Atlantic portion of the East Coast where the long arms of the Atlantic Ocean reach far into the coastal lands. It is in this area that European colonists first established a colony in North America with the founding of Jamestown in the spring of 1607.

Although these bodies of water may also be called rivers, they are affected by ocean tides. That is how the Tidewater area got its name. The Tidewater gave its colonists many advantages over other areas of the Atlantic coast in colonial times.

- The Delaware and Chesapeake Bays and their tributaries, such as the Potomac and James Rivers, allowed sailing ships to move cargo far inland. The rivers were deep enough that any village or plantation on its banks could easily build a wooden pier to load and unload cargo from the ships. This meant that the ships were not limited to deep-water ports like those in New England.
- In the days when roads were few and very poor, the ability to move cargo by water gave products from the Tidewater a trading advantage over other areas where products had to move to ports over land. That's why the Tidewater areas led the way in selling products such as tobacco, cotton, and grain, or raw materials like timber.
- Another advantage of living in the Tidewater area was that the winters were usually mild because it was so close to the water. Snow would rarely stay on the ground long.

But there were also disadvantages. During the summer, mosquitoes and other insects were everywhere, making life nearly unbearable at times, as well as unhealthy. Mosquitoes carried diseases like the dreaded yellow fever that could wipe out whole families. Other illnesses caused the premature deaths of many children. Life was often short and tragic.

Tobacco was grown throughout the Tidewater area and was often shipped to English merchants. The leaves were cut when green and then slowly cured under shelter.

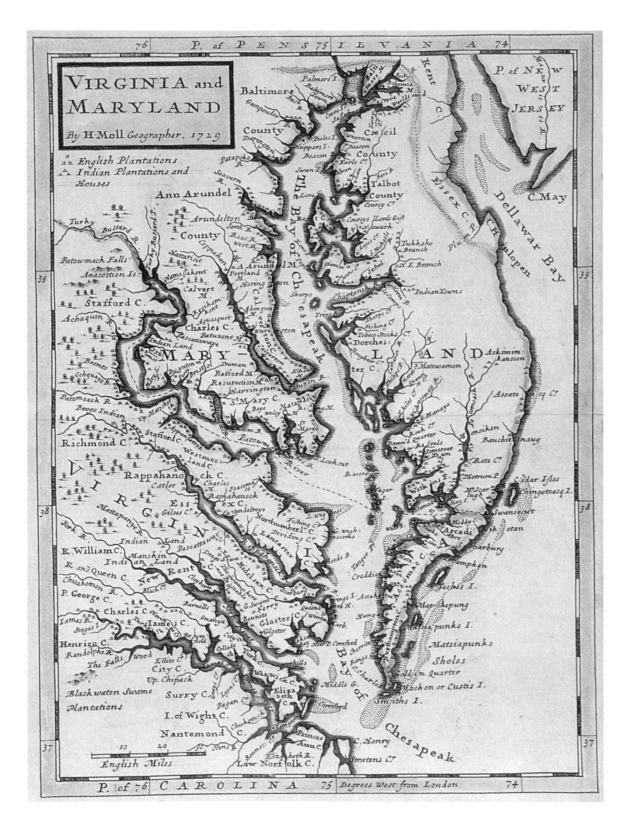

VIRGINIA and MARYLAND

By H·Moll Geographer, 1729

ᵃᵃ English Plantations
⌂ Indian Plantations and
Houses

16

The area just west of the Tidewater was known as the Piedmont. In Italian, *Piedmonte* means "foot of the mountain." The colonists began to move inland to the foothills as the coastal lands became more populated. The Piedmont's rolling hills and large flat areas proved to be rich land for farming, and many forms of agriculture soon prospered.

INDIAN RELATIONS

When the first colonial settlements were established more than a hundred years before Jed's time, American Indians were the only ones living in the Tidewater area. Why were they called Indians? Because when Christopher Columbus first discovered the Americas, he thought he'd sailed all the way to India. He did not realize he'd found America. So he called the people he met there Indians. Today these people are often called "Native Americans" because they lived on the North American continent for thousands of years before the colonists.

Many Indian words have lingered on as place names today. Delaware, Potomac, Susquehanna, and Roanoke are tribal names that you may recognize as rivers in the Tidewater region. Other tribes found in the area were the Choptank, Assateague, Tuscarora, Mattaponi, and the Pawmunkey.

Many of the English colonists in Virginia considered the Indians to be savages and refused to learn farming practices from them. To these colonists, the Indians were competitors for the fertile lands to the west. Most believed the only solution was to force the Indians off these fertile lands. But some colonists took a more cooperative attitude toward the Indians, who then taught them the hill-and-hoe method of gardening. The Indians would pile dirt up in an ankle-high hill, insert a dead fish in the middle of the hill, then plant their seeds on top of the fish. As the fish decayed, it provided food for the plant. This was a very useful farming practice because it worked well in fields which had been only partially cleared.

Maize, or corn, was probably the greatest contribution of the Indians to the colonists, but tobacco was a crucial gift. By the mid-1750s, tobacco was the biggest export item of the Tidewater, although wheat was also important. Further south in South Carolina and Georgia, rice was the popular crop.

As more and more colonists took ships across the Atlantic Ocean to the American colonies, competition for land and natural resources greatly increased. New diseases introduced by Europeans caused a great number of deaths among the Native Americans. By the mid-1700s, this combination had pushed the Indians west of the Allegheny Mountains on the western boundary of the rich Shenandoah Valley in Virginia.

Above, a one-room schoolhouse built in the early 1800s at Valley Forge, Pennsylvania. At left, a quill pen, created from a feather, with several of George Washington's books.

Chapter 2

School in 1750

FEBRUARY 22, 1750
LATER THAT MORNING

Jed kicked off his wooden clogs and slipped on his leather shoes for school. His shoes, when new, were not shaped to fit either foot. As he wore them, the leather shaped itself to the individual foot. They had been made by a slave named Dodd who belonged to their closest neighbor, Mr. Franklin. He was a cobbler or shoemaker. He cut and sewed leather made from the hides of farm animals into shoes for many people in the area.

Jed was lucky that he lived only about a mile from the small village of Stanley Hundred. It had an Anglican parish church with a school. The Anglican church was the official state church back in Great Britain. It took Jed less than half an hour to walk to school in the morning. Stanley Hundred had been established 123 years earlier, in 1627 by English settlers.

As Jed approached the village, he could see the church steeple above the trees which lined the rutted road ahead.

When he got to the edge of town, there were a few cabins, much like his own, scattered through the woods. Closer to the town's center, the houses were larger and made of brick.

In the very center of town, a large area had been left open at the intersection of the main roads. This was the town square. Around this were clustered the church, an inn which provided rooms and meals for visitors, and the general store.

The church bell was ringing to signal the start of school. Jed hurried to take his seat in the schoolroom attached on the side of the large church sanctuary.

INSIDE SCHOOL

The schoolroom had a fireplace on the side of one wall. The teacher sat at a desk on a small raised platform at the far end of the room. In front of this desk were wooden benches with long tilted desks. The younger children sat in front, the older ones in back. There were usually about twenty children in the room, ranging in age from seven to fifteen, all talking, laughing, and teasing one another in a noisy hubbub.

Mr. Johnson, the teacher, was about the age of Jed's father. He was a tall, thin man who wore glasses that were always slipping down his nose. In one hand he carried a five-foot birch rod about the thickness of Jed's finger. In his other hand, he clasped a book to his chest. He stood up and rapped on the desk with the birch rod.

"Quiet!" he thundered.

The room was instantly silent. All the children, even the oldest and biggest, respected Mr. Johnson's birch rod. It was a tool of many uses – used sometimes to get children's attention – sometimes as a pointer to single out a child to answer a question – but most often to give a rap across the knuckles of a child who was dozing off. Children guilty of more serious infractions would merit sharper strokes to their legs or buttocks.

Mr. Johnson opened the book at a marker where he had stopped reading the day before. "We will continue with the life of Alexander the Great," he announced. He cleared his throat.

"Once upon a time, Philonicus the Thessalian brought a beautiful horse named Bucephalus to King Philip of Greece. He offered to sell Bucephalus. When they took Bucephalus into the field to try him, they found him so very

It is likely that this small building in the upper garden at Mount Vernon was once used as a schoolroom for Martha Washington's grandchildren. It has just enough room for two young students and a tutor.

A typical fork and knife from the 18th century, probably used by George Washington.

vicious and unmanageable that he reared up when they endeavored to mount him, and would not so much as endure the voice of any of Philip's attendants. Finally, they gave up. As they started to lead him away, young Alexander spoke up. 'What an excellent horse do they lose for lack of boldness to manage him!' Alexander had noticed that the horse was afraid of its own shadow. He tamed Bucephalus by mounting him with his head facing the sun. This way the horse could not see his shadow, which caused him to be calm."

Mr. Johnson went on reading from the book called The Lives of the Noble Grecians and Romans *by someone named Plutarch. Jed enjoyed hearing about Alexander as a boy and about how he tamed the horse Bucephalus. Last year, when he listened to the deeds of great men of the past, he often had trouble following the stories. But Jed was understanding more this year. He*

saw some of the younger students beginning to fidget and knew that it wouldn't be long before Mr. Johnson's rod would swish down on whichever one caught his eye.

After reading for a little longer, Mr. Johnson closed the book and rapped the birch rod loudly on his desk. "Now, we will have the first group's recitation."

Four students, three of the youngest and a boy older than Jed, stood up and moved to the front row of benches. Mr. Johnson handed them books and then sat down at his desk. The students read a few lines each, then practiced spelling a few words. Jed always enjoyed the spelling because he was very good at it. Of course the younger students couldn't read very well, but they learned faster by being around the older ones.

As the first group read, the others picked up their slates and chalk and began to copy down the words being spelled out. Slates were thin pieces of smooth stone, a little smaller than a piece of today's writing paper, which could be written on. They were similar to small blackboards. Writing and ciphering were practiced on a slate. The student would scratch on the slate with another scrap of slate, a slate "pencil," or a piece of chalk. The writing was faint but legible, and could be erased with a piece of cloth or the heel of the student's hand.

MEALTIME

At noon, after all the students had taken turns doing their morning recitations, Mr. Johnson stood up. "It's time to eat." The students who lived in the village ran home to eat. Jed found a place to sit under the trees near the school. The late winter sun had warmed the air considerably.

Most of the children pulled pieces of hard bread or meat from their pockets or cloth bags. Jed's friend, Frank Hatch, sat down next to him. He pulled a piece of cornbread and a chunk of ham from a leather pouch that hung around his shoulder and began eating

A colonial placesetting: two horn cups and a period knife and fork shown atop a wooden "dish."

it. Soon they were joined by another friend, Willie Baker.

"My dog had pups last night," Frank beamed. "My dad said I could keep one, but I've got to find something to do with the other four. Would you like one, Jed?"

"Sure!" exclaimed Jed. "My father says we need one to keep the deer out of the garden."

"How about you, Willie?"

"I'll ask," promised Willie. "But we already have three dogs, and I don't think my mother wants any more."

Jed finished the last crumbs of his cornbread. "Why don't we go down to the river?" The other boys agreed. They jumped up and ran the short distance to the bank of the mighty James River. The river seemed huge, as big as an ocean. The opposite shore, about three miles across the river, was so far away that you could see only a thin, dark line where the shore was.

"What do you think it's like over there?" Willie asked.

"Probably the same as here," laughed Frank. "And I bet there are three other boys over there looking our way wondering what it's like over here."

Jed started looking for some flat, smooth river stones. It was fun to see how many times you could make them skip across the water. Seven skips was considered very good. But before they had a chance to throw a single rock, they heard Mr. Johnson calling back his students.

The boys managed to slip into their seats as the last of the children streamed in. Mr. Johnson handed out copies of the New England Primer *and*

When his father asked whether his son had cut down the cherry tree, young George Washington said "yes, I cannot tell a lie." Although this may be a fable rather than a true story, George Washington followed the Rules of Civility *as best he could, and he was known for his lifelong honesty.*

the afternoon recitations began with a short poem:

> *He who ne'er learns his ABC's*
> *Forever will a Block-head be;*
> *But he who to his Book's inclin'd,*
> *Will soon a golden treasure find.*

When the entire group finished reading, it was time to go home. Jed couldn't wait to tell his father about Frank's new pups.

When he got back, Jed changed into his wooden work shoes. He worked at clearing the garden until it was almost too dark to see. Then he herded the sheep and goats into the lean-to. He put some fresh hay into the barn manger for the cattle and went back to the house. He wondered what he would call his new puppy.

SCHOOL WAS DIFFERENT

In most of the colonies, there was no requirement that children attend school in 1750. Many children learned what they needed to know at home, and, unless the family was wealthy, the chances were that most children grew up without being able to read and write. Where there were schools, they were not the kind a boy or girl today would recognize. As in Jed's parish school, the teacher was usually most concerned with discipline.

Few children had textbooks of their own. Most of the instruction consisted of reading the same short passages over

Children in the 18th century not only went to school, they also had to complete a number of chores. It is hard work grinding corn in a pestle, so the meal can be used for baking.

and over, and writing the texts out on their slates. In the classroom, there were never any maps, blackboards, or the sorts of things today's students take for granted. But in spite of the shortcomings, many students learned quite a lot in these primitive conditions.

GEORGE WASHINGTON'S EDUCATION

Now let's take a look at how the father of our country, George Washington, was educated. Often, well-to-do parents hired tutors to supplement or substitute for schoolhouse education. Some even sent their sons and daughters back to England for their education. For example, George Washington's older half-brothers, Lawrence and Augustine, were educated in England, but George himself had only a few years of American education. Still, he was so good at mathematics that by age seventeen he became a professional surveyor.

George Washington worked hard on his penmanship by copying brief rules of polite behavior from a book called *Rules of Civility*. Composed in 1595, some of these rules are just practical advice. Some are funny to us today. But some of them influenced Washington's life powerfully, and can help guide students today to successful lives. Here are just a few:

- Every action done in company ought to be done with some sign of respect to those that are present.
- When a man does all he can though it succeed not well, blame not him that did it.
- When you see a crime punished, you may be inwardly pleased; but...show pity to the offending sufferer.
- Do not laugh too much or too

These are some of the books that George Washington assembled in his library over a lifetime. Washington always regretted his lack of formal education, but he worked hard to learn about science, history, literature and farming by reading books. He was also a person who took the time to write hundreds of letters to friends and family.

loud in public.
- Drink not, nor talk with your mouth full.
- Cleanse not your teeth with the table cloth napkin, fork or knife.
- Kill no vermin [such] as fleas, lice, ticks, etc. in the sight of others.
- Bedew no man's face with your spittle.

It is common to see someone with young George's education write with many misspellings and punctuation errors. For example, when he was about 17 years old he wrote a friend about a surveying trip in the wilderness:

I have not sleep'd above three Nights or four in a bed but after Walking a good deal all the Day lay down before the fire upon a Little Hay Straw Fodder or bairskin which ever is to be had with Man Wife and Children like a Parcel of Dogs or Catts & happy's he that gets the Birth nearest the fire....

As he grew older, George Washington continued to improve his penmanship and writing skills, although even as an adult, he wished he had had a better education.

At left, a scene from a beach on the Potomac River, which was an important source of food and transportation. Above, a colonial woman places a heavy cast-iron pot over a cooking fire.

Chapter 3

Jed's Birthday Party

FEBRUARY 22, 1750
THE EVENING

Jed's mother and sister were in the kitchen when he went in. The room was warm and smelled wonderfully of wood smoke, baking pastry, and meat roasting.

"What smells so good?" Jed asked eagerly.

"We made a mince pie for your birthday," Abby replied. "It's made out of the venison from the deer Papa shot on Monday."

"Wash up now, Jed," his mother said sweetly. "Your father should be here any moment, and we are ready to eat."

Jed dipped a gourd full of water from a wooden bucket next to the fire into a hollowed-out wooden bowl and carried it to the table. He used a big spoonful of his mother's homemade soft soap on his face and hands, rinsed them, then dried them on a piece of rough toweling hanging near the fireplace. *His eyes stung when the strong lye from the wood ashes used to make the soap got into them.*

Jed's father came in just as his mother was taking the pie from the brick oven that was built into the side of the fireplace. "Mmm, that smells good. I'm hungry."

Mary Warwick brushed her long brown hair away from her face before she greeted her husband with a quick kiss. "Well, supper is ready right now, so you'd better wash up. Abby, you can get Jed's presents now."

Abby scampered to the fireplace and climbed on the bench set next to it. She reached up to the rafter overhead and retrieved a small package wrapped in paper and tied with string. After she put it at Jed's place at the table, everyone sat down. Jed's mother smiled at her firstborn. "All right. You can open it now."

As the paper slid off, he saw the cover of a copy of The New England Primer. *He opened it up and saw a picture of King George of England on the first page. "Thank you so much. This will make it a lot easier for me to study at home now. Mr. Johnson will be so surprised when I have to recite." He stood up and hugged each one of his family. Mary and Tom Warwick smiled at each other. Their son was growing up.*

Jed's mother sliced the pork roast and dished it onto the wooden plates stacked at her side. There was a pitcher of cider on the table, and they filled their cups with as much as they wanted. Jed's father spooned some potatoes and

carrots onto everyone's plate. *After the blessing, Jed excitedly told his father and mother about Frank's puppies. As he'd hoped, his father said he could pick one out as soon as they were old enough. They talked over the day's events as they ate.*

When they were all finished, Jed's mother brought the mince pie to the table and cut it into pieces and served it. "Happy birthday, Jed," his mother whispered as she bent over him and kissed him on the cheek.

"Thank you, Mama," Jed beamed.

"You really need to thank your sister, Jed. She was the one who made the pie."

Jed looked at Abby and saw her blushing. "I didn't know you could make pie like this, Abby," he teased.

"Mother showed me how. I chopped the dried apples and the venison and the raisins together, and Mother helped me with the pie crust. It's wasn't nearly as hard as I thought it would be," she smiled.

Tom Warwick smoothed his daughter's hair with a gentle hand. "Well, it's a good first pie. You should be very proud of it. Now, Jed, get out the checkers and we'll play a game before bed."

Jed went to the cabinet and took out a box and a wooden board with squares painted on it. He brought them to the table. They set up the board between them in front of the fire and placed the round playing pieces on alternating squares. Jed moved first.

Meanwhile, Abby and Mother cleared the table and washed the dishes before returning them to the rack near the cabinet on the side wall. Tom and Jed were quiet next to the warm, crackling fire.

Suddenly, Tom shook his head and looked up at his son as he slapped his thigh. "Ha!" he shouted "You've learned a lot this winter, Jed! You've got me beat."

Abby and her mother laughed. When Jed won, it had always seemed as though his father played the game to help him win. This time, it looked as if Jed had beaten him fair and square.

"Since I can't beat my own son anymore, I might as well turn in," Tom sighed.

Jed and Abby giggled, "Goodnight, Papa."

"You children need to go to bed, too," their mother said. "And happy birthday, Jed."

Jed and Abby hugged her. "Goodnight, mother."

Jed walked across the open porch and climbed the log ladder to his loft. The fireplace below sent light through cracks between the split logs that made up his floor. It lit the loft with a faint glow. He undressed quickly, pulled his nightshirt on, then climbed under the chilly covers, and sank deep into the soft mattress filled with feathers. It had

An early checker set.

been a wonderful birthday, and he was sure his next one would be even better. After all, he'd have a new dog to help him celebrate. He turned over and was asleep almost before he was settled in.

THE GEOGRAPHY OF NEW ENGLAND

The New England Colonies — those colonies to the north and east of present-day New York — were quite different from those in the Tidewater and the Piedmont. The difference came from the nature of the land and the climate, as well as the character of the region's settlers.

THE LAND

New England was not as easy to farm as the Tidewater and the Piedmont. Much of it was not only hilly and rocky, but also heavily forested. Farmers had to remove both the timber and the rocks before they could even begin farming. They used the stone they cleared from the land to build their field walls. That's why today you will see many more stone walls in New England than in other parts of the United States.

Land in New England is not as fertile as it is in the Tidewater or the Piedmont. The farmers had to be careful to choose crops that could grow in soil that was often poor and rocky. Fruit trees, berry vines, and vegetables were typically the best crops, though grain could be grown in some parts of New England. For this reason, much of

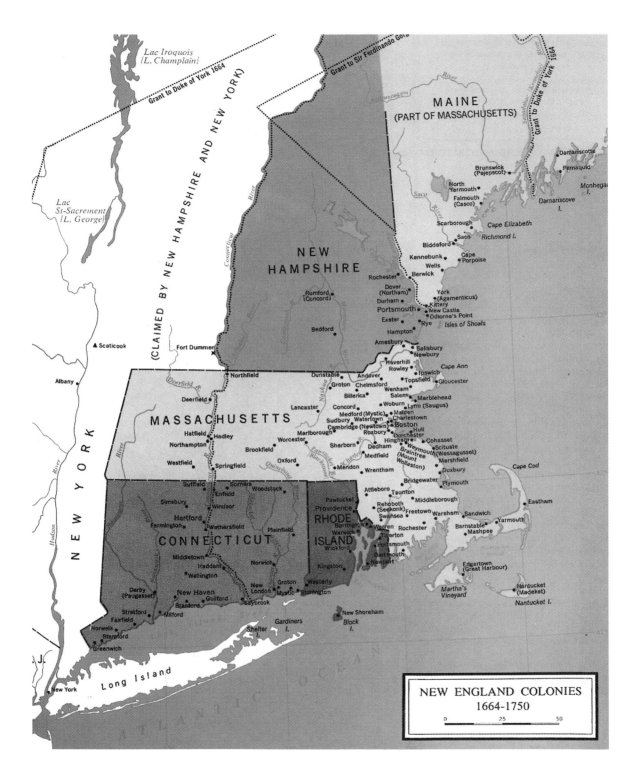

This map shows the colonies in New England, where the Pilgrims originally settled in 1620. By 1750, the four New England colonies had a population of 350,000 people.

30

the region was used for raising livestock, especially dairy cattle.

New England did not have the long arms of the Atlantic Ocean reaching inland like the Tidewater region did. Therefore, it was dependent on good harbors and ports to be able to conduct trade with England and the southern colonies. Large towns, which eventually became cities, formed around these harbors. They were larger than any of the cities in the Tidewater. In many of these harbors, important industries such as shipbuilding, fishing, and whaling developed over the years.

THE CLIMATE

New England has short, pleasant summers and long, cold winters. Colonists who settled in New England found that winter storms could be especially severe. They were forced to build stronger barns than were needed in the south to protect their livestock. Except for the effects of the cold weather, however, the climate was generally healthful. Many of the diseases which were common in the South were not a problem in the North because the colder winters killed off insects and other spreaders of disease. For this reason, the life expectancy in New England was longer than in the Tidewater or the Piedmont, so the population grew more rapidly.

THE SETTLERS

Many early settlers of New England came for religious reasons. The Puritans were the most famous, but there were other religious groups who settled in New England after fleeing persecution in Europe. For this reason, religious influences were more important in forming the character of New England than in the Tidewater or the Piedmont.

In the seventeenth century – the 1600s – the religious nature of the settlers of New England had a strong influence on the culture. Although everyone did not have to belong to a church, almost everyone was expected to attend church every Sunday. Fathers were the heads of their households. Even when their children were grown, fathers made many of the important decisions for them. Often, laws that the New England colonies passed had purely religious purposes.

Though slaves were present in New England, and many slave traders were New Englanders, slavery never grew there like it did in Virginia and other southern colonies. This was partly for religious reasons – the Shakers were opposed to slavery, and many Shakers lived in New England – but also New England had neither large plantations which required slave labor, nor a long growing season to justify keeping slaves through the long, cold winters. Still, in port towns, like Newport, Rhode Island, over 10% of the population were slaves by the 1700s.

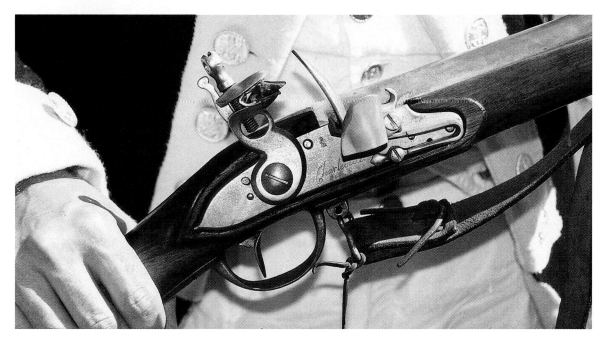

At left, George Washington at age 21 crossing the wintry Allegheny River on a raft fashioned with "one poor Hatchet." Due to ice in the river, Washington and his guide had to abandon the raft and swim to shore. Above, a classic American long rifle.

Chapter 4

The European Contest for America

The journeys of Christopher Columbus to the West Indies near the end of the fifteenth-century (late 1400s) sparked a competition among the great powers of Europe for control over the New World. The next 300 years of the history of North and South America is the story of struggles for dominance in Europe and in the Americas.

By 1700, the battle for North America had narrowed to three European nations: France, Spain, and Great Britain. France had laid claim to the largest land area in North America. France dominated what is now Canada and a wedge southward through the middle of today's United States. This wedge spread from today's Montana, east to New York, and south down the Mississippi River to Louisiana.

Spain was the next-largest land-holder. It controlled the islands of the Caribbean and what is now Florida. Northward, its territories extended through south Georgia and westward to what is today southern Alabama and Mississippi.

Great Britain's land holdings were the smallest. They included the eastern seaboard of the United States from

George Washington's first job was that of a surveyor of the western territory. This helped him to learn more about the land where many battles would be fought in the French and Indian War.

today's Maine to mid-Georgia, and territories stretching inland for 200-300 miles. Although the Dutch had been the first settlers in the New York area, which they called New Amsterdam, the English had replaced them by 1700.

FRENCH AND INDIAN WAR

Conflicts between the European powers in North America were few before 1700. There were two important reasons for this:

- There was enough land with plentiful natural resources to send back to each country.
- The European countries were occupied with struggles within their own borders, and also with problems concerning the European continent.

By the beginning of the 18th century, however, these conditions had changed. From 1688 to 1763, the English and the French would fight four wars in North America. The final war actually started in North America in 1754 and spread to Europe two years later. In North America, this war was called the French and Indian War. In Europe, it was called the Seven Years War because it lasted from 1756 to 1763. After the defeat of France in this war, Great Britain dominated what would eventually become the United States.

The spark that started the French and Indian War was rivalry over the rich lands along the Ohio River. British colonists wanted the right to expand beyond the Appalachian Mountains. But the French were determined to prevent them from doing so. Each side had alliances with Indian tribes to help them fight against the other.

FIRST CLASH

In the early 1750s, a group of wealthy Virginians formed a company and secured a huge grant of land in the Ohio River Valley from the British king. Called the Ohio Company, it intended to divide the land into small farms and then sell the farms to settlers. For many years the French had claimed this land. Though there were no settlers in the area, the French had built a few scattered forts to support their claim. With news of the Virginians' plan, the French got busy. They constructed a string of forts connecting Lake Erie with the Ohio River.

Meanwhile, back in Virginia, the investors didn't like the news of the French forts. They decided to send a warning to the French. In 1753, a 21-year-old surveyor named George Washington volunteered to carry the message. He had recently become an officer in the Virginia militia. In those days all able-bodied men served in the militia with a few exceptions, such as ministers.

Washington had become an apprentice surveyor at age sixteen when he had helped map out the fertile Shenandoah Valley. By age seventeen, he was a self-employed surveyor, a job which could be very profitable. It was one of the few professions which was paid in cash. Most people were paid in tobacco in that day in Virginia. Young Washington was a hard worker, and he saved his money carefully. When he saw a good piece of land for sale, he'd buy it. By age twenty-one, young Washington was already a big land owner. He owned about 2,300 acres of land.

The warning from the Governor of Virginia, Robert Dinwiddie, said that the British had given the Ohio River Valley to the Ohio Company, and the French must not interfere. In October of 1753, Washington set out on horseback to contact the French. With him was a small group of men – a guide, an interpreter, and four frontiersmen.

WASHINGTON REJECTED

In mid-November, Washington's party stopped at an Indian village at the site of present-day Pittsburgh. There, three Indian chiefs agreed to accompany Washington. They gave him a warrior's name meaning "Towntaker." In early December, young Washington reached French headquarters to deliver Dinwiddie's warning, which was promptly rejected. The French commander gave Washington a letter to carry back to the Governor.

Washington returned to Williamsburg in January to deliver the letter to Governor Dinwiddie. He also urged the Governor to quickly build a fort where the Monongahela and Allegheny Rivers join to become the Ohio River – where Washington had first met the Indians. The Governor immediately sent a party of frontiersmen to build the fort. He also promoted Washington to Lieutenant Colonel and ordered him to recruit troops to man the new fort.

JUNE 1, 1754

The mill house was still shrouded in shadow and dripping with early morning dew. As he did every morning, Jed opened the gate that diverted the water from the millpond over to the huge water wheel. The 20-foot diameter wooden wheel groaned and shuddered as it began to turn. Before long, the whole millhouse was rumbling with the vibrations of the wooden wheels and gears that drove the machinery of the mill.

Jed was happy. It was good to be working in the new mill on such a beautiful, summer day. He didn't mind the

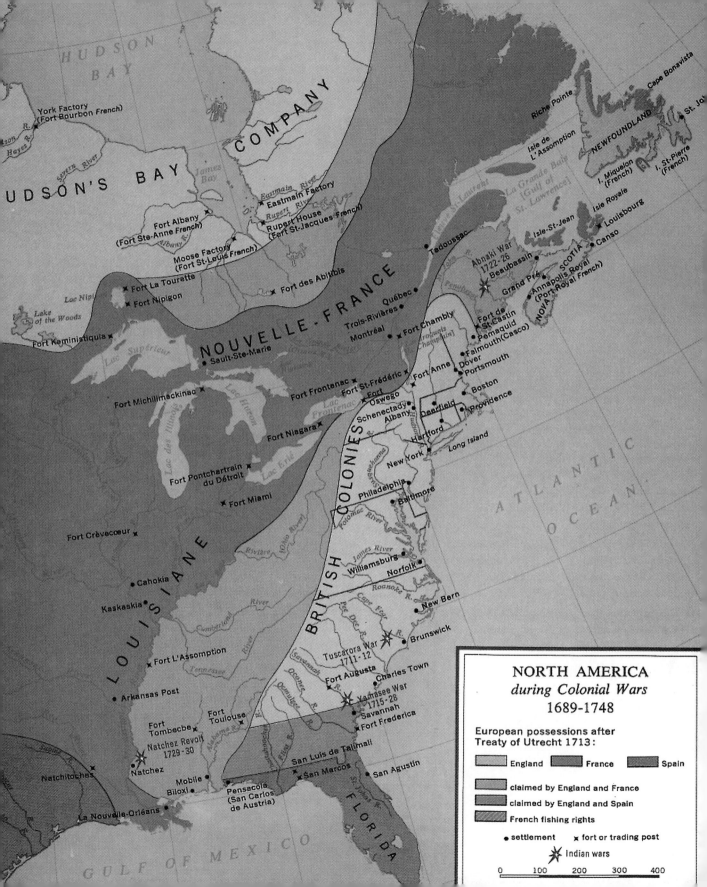

HUDSON BAY

HUDSON'S BAY

COMPANY

York Factory
(Fort Bourbon French)

Severn River

Hayes R.

James Bay

Eastmain Factory

Rupert River

Rupert House
(Fort St-Jacques French)

Fort Albany
(Fort Ste-Anne French)

Albany R.

Moose Factory
(Fort St-Louis French)

Fort La Tourette

Fort des Abitibis

Fort Nipigon

Lac Nipi

Lake
of the Woods

Lac Supérieur

Fort Keministiquia

NOUVELLE-FRANCE

Sault-Ste-Marie

Lac Huron

Fort Michillimackinac

Lac des Illinois

Fort Frontenac

Lac Frontenac

Fort St-Frédéric

Fort
Oswego

Fort Niagara

Lac Érié

Fort Pontchartrain
du Détroit

Fort Miami

Ohio River

Rivière

Fort Crèvecoeur

LOUISIANE

Cahokia

Kaskaskia

River

Cumberland River

Fort L'Assomption

Tennessee

Arkansas Post

Natchez Revolt
1729-30

Natchitoches

Natchez

Fort
Tombecbe

Alabama R.

Fort
Toulouse

Mobile

Biloxi

Pensacola
(San Carlos
de Austria)

La Nouvelle-Orléans

GULF OF MEXICO

Riche Pointe

Cape Bonavista

Isle de
L'Assomption

NEWFOUNDLAND

St. Joh

I. Miquelon
(French)

I. St-Pierre
(French)

Fleuve St-Laurent

La Grande Baie
(Gulf of
St. Lawrence)

Tadoussac

Abnaki War
1722-26

Beaubassin

Isle-St-Jean

Isle Royale

Louisbourg

Canso

Grand Pré

NOVA SCOTIA

Annapolis Royal
(Port-Royal French)

Québec

Trois-Rivières

Montréal

Fort Chambly

Fort de
St-Castin

Pemaquid

Lac
Champlain

Iroquois

Falmouth(Casco)

Fort Anne

Dover

Portsmouth

Schenectady

Albany

Fort
Deerfield

Boston

Providence

Hartford

Hudson R.

New York

Long Island

BRITISH COLONIES

Philadelphia

Susquehanna R.

Baltimore

Potomac River

James River

Williamsburg

Norfolk

Roanoke R.

Cape Fear

Pee Dee R.

New Bern

Tuscarora War
1711-12

Brunswick

Savannah R.

Fort Augusta

Ocon

Charles Town

Yamasee War
1715-28

Savannah

Fort Frederica

San Luis de Talimali

San Marcos

San Agustin

St. John R.

FLORIDA

ATLANTIC

OCEAN

NORTH AMERICA
during Colonial Wars
1689-1748

European possessions after
Treaty of Utrecht 1713:

England ▭   France ▭   Spain ▭

▭ claimed by England and France

▭ claimed by England and Spain

▨ French fishing rights

● settlement   ✕ fort or trading post

✴ Indian wars

0   100   200   300   400

The Battle of Monongahela was a crushing defeat for the colonists and the British, who were forced to retreat when attacked by the French and Indians, who hid behind trees. But Washington learned lessons from this defeat that would help him in his long and important military career. At left, a map of the British colonies in North America.

hard work. He didn't even mind the fact that he and his mother and sister would have to run it all by themselves while his father was with Lieutenant Colonel Washington on an expedition to the Ohio territory.

He just wished his mother didn't miss his father so terribly. She didn't understand why men would ride hundreds of miles just to get into a fight — especially when they had a family and a business to attend to.

Jed missed his father, too. He thought back to the early spring morning when he had left. Tom Warwick had laid his arm across his son's shoulders.

"Jed, you're going to be the man of the family while I'm gone. It's going to be your responsibility to take care of your mother and sister until I get back. I can earn enough money just this summer to pay off almost everything we owe on the mill. But it all depends on you, son. Do you think you can handle it? There are animals to take care of, and the garden, and the mill on top of that."

Jed nodded silently. He was a little bit scared, but he was also proud of his father's trust. His friend, Frank Hatch, was in the same fix. His father was also marching with Lieutenant Colonel Washington. At age thirteen, both boys were going to be the man of their house for the summer.

"You do everything your mother asks you to without complaint or having to be told twice," his father continued. "I'm leaving my old musket for you and taking my new one. You can shoot some rabbits and squirrels to help your mother with the food. But your main job will be running the mill. Mr. Franklin will help you when he can, but it's your responsibility. I don't know how long I'll be gone. I expect I'll be back before fall. But you're not to worry about me, all right?"

Jed nodded silently. He knew what to do. He'd worked beside his father at the mill for the last four years. That's just the way it was. Boys grew up into men by the time they were teenagers in the Tidewater.

His father handed Jed the heavy old musket, the wooden ramrod sticking out just a little past the long metal barrel. Once again – just to be sure – he showed his son how to push the hammer forward, put a little powder in the metal pan below the hammer, close the hammer, pull the cock back and then pull the trigger. The flint stone bolted into the hammer, smashed down, struck the frissen and caused sparks which ignited the powder in the pan. W-H-O-O-S-H! flashed the powder in the pan in smoke and flame.

Then he showed the boy how to put more powder down the barrel, followed by a leaden ball, packing it tight against the bottom with the ramrod. All this took about half a minute.

"Next time you put powder in the pan and shoot, something will come out. Don't forget to aim a little high. The ball doesn't carry much more than a hundred yards," pointing across a field in front of the house.

****

His mother's voice broke into his thoughts. "Jed, the Tidwell's corn is in barrels by the mill," she yelled over the rumble of the mill wheel. "Can you get it ground before lunch? Mr. Tidwell would like to come for it this afternoon."

"I'll have it done by mid-morning," Jed answered. "I'm going to get it started, then catch some fish for lunch."

"If you do, give them to Abby to clean and fry. I'm going to be too busy to do it myself."

Jed adjusted the mill for corn and pulled the rope that started it turning. Then he poured the bags of corn into a trough that would slowly feed it between the huge round millstones. He waited until he saw the meal start to sift out of the bottom of the mill, then grabbed his cane fishing pole and ran to the door.

"Come on, Wooley," Jed called to his dog. "We've got to hurry if we're gonna catch a fish or two before that corn is ground." Wooley was one of the puppies Frank Hatch had given him four years ago. Now he was a big dog. His head was as high as Jed's waist. He and Jed were constant companions.

Jed picked up an old bucket. He and his father used it to scoop out bait minnows from Skiffes Creek, which fed the millpond. When he'd trapped a half-dozen minnows in the bucket, he carried it out onto the small wooden pier he and his father had built. He sat down and baited his hook. Wooley lay down in the sun on the warm wooden planks and immediately went to sleep.

As Jed tossed the fishing line into the water and watched the ripples circle out around the cork he used for a bobber, he thought again about his father on the frontier. He'd heard nothing for three months since his dad had left. A day never went by without Jed remembering his father's last words to him as he walked him to the mill on that crisp March morning when he had left.

Jed was still thinking about that last day with his father when he saw the cork twitch. Instantly he was alert, gripping the pole tightly. When the cork went under, he yanked the line and pulled in a nice-sized fish. Wooley woke up and wagged his tail excitedly as he sniffed the fish flopping on the dock. Jed removed the hook, then put a willow branch through the fish's gill and out its mouth. He then carefully put the branch and the fish back into the water to stay fresh.

Before long, Jed had half a dozen fish on the branch. Some people called them bream fish, but Jed just called them "bluegills" because of the fish's bright blue gill covers. Most were small, the size of Jed's hand, but he also had two large ones, almost as big as his two hands together.

Coopering, or making barrels, was an important job in colonial times, because hundreds of barrels were needed to ship flour, corn, tobacco and household goods.

He carried them to the house and left them on the back porch. He and his father had built a new house last year. Made of brick and stone, it was a handsome dwelling, two stories high, with an attic and cellar. It was laid out like most houses of that time and place, with four big rooms downstairs and four more upstairs. A wide hall ran from front to back, on both floors, to allow as much cool air to circulate during the summertime as possible.

"Abby, there's some fish on the porch for lunch," Jed called into the house. "Did you hear me? I've gotta get back to the mill."

"All right. Just leave them outside," Abby called out through an upstairs window.

Jed got back just as the last of the corn was feeding in between the large mill stones his father had imported all

Sheep were important sources of wool to make clothes and food for the table.

40

The Colvin Run Mill near Great Falls, Virginia, is one of the few remaining working mills in the country.

the way from France. He pulled the rope to stop the stone from turning, then began sifting the coarse-ground meal through a horsehair sieve. The sifted meal fell into a small wooden barrel. Jed looked over at another barrel next to a set of scales. This barrel was filled with corn that he had taken from the Tidwell's corn. By law, a miller had a right to one-eighth of a farmer's grain in return for grinding it. It was a good system. The owner got his corn ground without having to pay cash to the mill. The mill owner could either use the corn for his own food or sell it to people who did not grow their own.

Suddenly, Jed heard his mother calling outside.

"I've got the Tidwell's meal finished," he yelled out.

His mother gave him a hug as she came in. "Fine, Jed. That's the only job we have today. This afternoon, you better start grinding some of that wheat up in the loft. We've had lots of customers buying flour lately, and we're getting pretty low."

Jed made a face. He didn't like making wheat flour because it was slower and more work than grinding corn. It had to be ground twice, and the sifting process was tedious. But he remembered his father's words – "without complaint or having to be told twice." He nodded and smiled at his mother. "I'll get started right after lunch."

Above, Fort Necessity, 11 miles east of Uniontown, Pennsylvania, built by Colonel George Washington in 1754 as a defense against an approaching French force. Here, 393 men commanded by Washington were surrounded by a force of about 600 French troops and 100 Indians. Burned by the French, Fort Necessity was reconstructed on the original site in 1954. At left, a portrait of Washington in the uniform of colonel of The Virginia Regiment.

Chapter 5

Fort Necessity

In April 1754, 22-year-old George Washington set out as the second-in-command of an expedition to man the new fort at the forks of the Ohio River with about 160 poorly trained soldiers. As he approached the fort, he learned it had recently been captured before it was finished by the French, who had then named it Fort Duquesne.

On May 28, Washington's troops surprised a group of French troops, killed ten men and took 21 prisoners, while losing only one soldier themselves. This was Washington's first taste of battle and instead of finding it frightening, he found it exciting. He later wrote: "I heard the bullets whistle, and believe me there is something charming in the sound."

Washington decided to build a fort about 50 miles south of Fort Duquesne, while he waited for reinforcements from Virginia. He called it Fort Necessity.

AUGUST 1, 1754

Jed was down in the basement of the mill house that steamy August morning.

A private in the Virginia Regiment. Painting by Don Troiani.

He had shut the mill down because it seemed to be making more noise than usual. His father had taught him never to let odd noises persist in the mill without finding out what was causing them.

He had gone over all the machinery but had not found any places with unusual wear showing on the mostly wooden parts. So he walked down to Mr. Franklin's place and asked him to look at the machinery with him. After they had gone over everything, they decided that the unusual vibrations were probably the result of the wood drying out in the hot summer weather. Jed found a mallet and pounded a flat piece of wood, called a shim, into the space that had opened due to the shrinking mill parts.

Suddenly, he heard his mother scream. Frightened, he quickly climbed out of the millrace and ran around to the front of the mill. There was a strange horse tied in front. A man in buckskins was holding his mother tightly. Jed started toward him, more than a little afraid. Before he reached them, however, the man turned around. Jed's eyes widened when he recognized his father. He looked so different. He was leaner and tanned and had a short beard, and his left arm was in a sling.

His father smiled. "Jed, don't tell me you didn't recognize me either? You look like you've seen a ghost."

Jed nearly broke down in tears as he leapt to hug his father. He noticed how much older he looked. The wilderness takes its toll on a man, he thought.

"It's great to have you back, Papa. Are you back for good?"

"I think so. At least until they need to raise a militia again. And anyway, I'm not going anywhere until this shoulder finally heals up."

Both Jed and his mother looked at the makeshift bandage and winced in sympathy.

"Don't worry, you two. It's not as bad as it looks. A ball grazed me. I was lucky. I've seen others die from wounds like this that didn't take to healing."

"How did it happen, Papa?"

"I'll tell you soon enough. Just let me get out of these buckskins and into some of my clothes first."

Mary Warwick wiped away her tears with her apron.

"Jed, go kill a chicken for Abby to stew for supper."

Jed ran back to the house as fast as he could. "Abby, Abby, guess what..."

That night, Tom thought he'd never tasted a chicken stew as good as Abby had prepared. Finally, Jed couldn't stand the suspense any more. "Papa, tell me about it, please!"

Slowly Tom finished his last spoonful of the delicious stew. "We got beat. We did all we could, but the French and their Indians ran us out of our fort. Colonel Washington moved about fifty miles away to a place called Great Meadows and built a fort we called Fort Necessity."

Mary Warwick was busy cutting a piece of fresh black raspberry pie for her husband. He thanked her and smiled warmly before he dug in. "This is delicious, Mary. You don't know how many times I dreamed about eating your pie. You really don't realize what you've got until you start missing it."

Jed couldn't stand the delay. "Well, come on. Tell me more."

"Jed, I'll tell you, I've never worked harder in my life or been more tired than I was trying to build that fort. There were more mosquitoes than I've ever seen. We were in bottom land along a creek. It would have made a great farm and a mill, but it was a terrible place for a fort.

"We didn't have enough of anything. And we wouldn't have had anything at all without Colonel Washington. He's a fine young officer. Took care of us as best he could, but with not enough flour or even wagons to carry supplies, there wasn't much he could do. Luckily we drove enough cattle with us to have fresh beef, but not much else.

"It was on the morning of July 3 that the sentries saw the Indians across the meadow. They started shooting and we all turned out for a fight, but the sergeants told us to hold our fire. At first, it was raining – just lightly, but then buckets full of water, it seemed like. The trenches soon filled with water, and we were knee-deep in mud inside the fort. Colonel Washington passed the word to keep our powder dry, but there wasn't much anyone could do.

"By evening time, the French had shot everything that moved – every cow and horse, and even every dog we had. We took a lot of casualties. It was terrible. They wanted to leave us with no food and no pack animals. Finally word was passed to open fire. We shot some of them, but didn't know how many. By dark, everyone's powder was damp and *no one was shooting anymore. That's when we heard them calling out across the meadow – calling and calling – calling in French for us to give up. We couldn't understand much of what they said.*

"That night, we all got little sleep, standing in fighting positions throughout the night. Colonel Washington saw we were in bad shape and figured we had better try to work out surrender terms so we could get out of there alive. We surrendered the fort the next morning.

"By mid-morning, we packed up whatever we could carry, formed up to the drums beating, and marched out with our flags flying high. We got to keep our muskets to fight off Indians on the way home. Although nobody felt much like a parade, we were all thankful that no one else was going to die in that muddy mess," recounted Tom Warwick.

"How many did you lose?" Jed asked in a quiet voice.

"About a hundred, counting killed and ones wounded like me. Would have been many, many more without Colonel Washington's discipline. He made everybody keep up – no stragglers."

"What's Colonel Washington like, Papa?" asked Abby.

"Big man, over six feet tall. Biggest in the unit. Strong, too. Rarely laughs. Seldom smiles. Keeps his mouth closed most of the time. When he talks, it's serious sounding. He looks like a soldier in that blue and red coat. Sits tall in the saddle and walks erect, just like an Indian. I don't think there was a man

who didn't respect him – for sure by the time it was over.

"He came by and checked the wounded every day. Those who couldn't keep up were given a helping hand. Some of them we even carried."

Tom Warwick looked tired. The lines in his lean and leathery cheeks had grown deeper in the telling of his story.

"Children, your father needs to rest. And so do you. Off to bed," said mother.

"We're glad you're home, Papa," Abby said. She threw her arms around him for a goodnight hug and kiss. As they climbed the wide stairway, Jed whispered, "Papa looks worn out, doesn't he, Abby?"

"Yes, but he doesn't look sick. We can nurse him back to being fit as a fiddle in no time at all."

FRANKLIN PROPOSES UNITING THE COLONIES

As a result of Washington's defeat at Fort Necessity, the American colonies were exposed to attack from the French and the Indians. To discuss ways to deal with this threat, delegates from seven of the colonies met in Albany, New York, along with their Indian allies, the six major Iroquois tribes known as the Six Nations. At the meeting, Benjamin Franklin first proposed that the colonies would be stronger if they united. Franklin's proposal of 1754, known as the Albany Plan of Union, was rejected. The colonists feared that if they united, they would lose their right to act

The structures inside the barricade at Fort Necessity were simple and easy to build in a brief period of time.

independently. But even though it failed, the Albany Plan was the first attempt to unite the colonies.

BRADDOCK'S DEFEAT

When Washington returned home from Fort Necessity, he decided to rent the estate of his recently deceased half-brother, Lawrence, from his widow, Ann, and become a farmer. He agreed to rent Mount Vernon for 15,000 pounds of tobacco a year. But the next spring, Washington received a message from Major General Edward Braddock of the regular British Army. He asked Washington if he would accompany him for an attack on the French-held Fort Duquesne. Washington agreed. He thought it would be an excellent opportunity to learn military tactics and organization from an experienced general.

During the march, Washington became seriously ill with a high fever. He warned Braddock that the tactics used by the French and their Indian allies in the forests of America were very different from those Braddock knew from the battlefields of Europe. Wearing bright red uniforms, 1,300 British soldiers marched through the unbroken wilderness in long straight columns. They looked as though they were on parade before the King.

Fearing the worst, Washington

A letter written by General Braddock just weeks before he died on the battlefield.

ordered his men to take him from his sickbed and put him on his horse with pillows tied to the saddle. Braddock was confident that the French would wait inside their fort for his assault so he ignored Washington's advice and called in his scouts and guards as they drew closer to Fort Dusquesne. But the French surprised him. About 300 French and Indians attacked unexpectedly. Their attack was so swift that the British troops, according to Washington, "broke and ran as sheep before the hounds."

General Braddock was killed, but Washington was miraculously uninjured. He would later write, "I luckily escaped without a wound, though I had four bullets through my coat and two horses shot under me...."

Washington returned home to Virginia again in the summer of 1755, disappointed in his military career so far. As he put it: "I have been on the losing order ever since I entered the service."

A French Retreat

In August of 1758, Governor Dinwiddie persuaded Washington to lead a regiment of regular soldiers to help try to take Fort Duquesne again. This time the force would be under the command of the British General John Forbes. But before Washington and the British could get there, the French burned the fort and retreated northward to Canada. To the French, the retreat was due at least partially to the fact that they were running low on supplies. Washington was disappointed that the French retreated, but he and his soldiers celebrated it as a great victory, anyway. Now, at only age 26, George Washington was the most famous American-born soldier.

The next year, 1759, the British won sweeping victories over the French, including the capture of the fortress at Quebec in what is now Canada. That year, the British Empire triumphed over her enemies in Europe, India, and the Mediterranean. In fact, British historians referred to 1759 as "the wonderful year."

By 1762, Spain feared the British would take over the entire world, so they entered the global conflict on the side of France. But Spain was too late. The British continued to win great victories. At a peace conference in 1763, Britain, Spain, and France finally agreed to stop fighting. Called the Treaty of Paris, the agreement gave Great Britain all of North America east of the Mississippi River, except the city of New Orleans. The treaty also gave Canada to the British, as well as all of France's holdings in India. Spain had to give up Florida to the British but in exchange got the vast unexplored territory west of the Mississippi River.

Although the American colonies were far from being united, they had gained military experience. Equally important, they had learned that they had to cooperate if they hoped to defend themselves. The stage was now set for the revolt against Great Britain that would give the colonies their independence.

Above, George Washington was one of early America's most creative and successful farmers. He invented a new plow, designed a remarkable 16-sided barn, and devised his own seven-year crop rotation. At left, Mount Vernon corn crops await harvest.

Chapter 6

Washington, The Gentleman Farmer

After his successful mission to chase the French from Fort Duquesne in the winter of 1758, the threat to Virginians subsided and George Washington returned to Mount Vernon. Though only 26, young Washington was highly respected. For example, while he was still on the frontier, he had been elected to the Virginia House of Burgesses.

On January 6, 1759, he married a widow, Martha Custis. Her first husband had left Martha and her two children a fortune in cash, about 17,000 acres of land, and many slaves. Washington became a loving stepfather, although he and Martha would have no children of their own.

Washington traveled from Mount Vernon to Williamsburg, then the capital of Virginia, when the colonial legislature met. During the next 15 years, he was re-elected many times. It was here he met important Virginia leaders such as Thomas Jefferson and Patrick Henry.

Washington was one of the quieter members of the Virginia legislature. He rarely spoke and did not introduce any important bills. But slowly, his fellow members in the House of Burgesses got to know this quiet young man from Northern Virginia. They respected his opinions and sought out his advice.

Much has been written about how Washington's appearance commanded respect. His soldiers could pick him out from his aides at a distance by the way he sat on his horse. In 1760, Washington's aide in the French and Indian War, Captain George Mercer, wrote a description of him:

[He is as] straight as an Indian, measuring six feet two inches in his stockings and weighing 175 pounds.... His frame is padded with well-developed muscles, indicating great strength.... He is wide shouldered but has not a deep or round chest; is neat waisted, but is broad across the hips and has rather long legs and arms. His head is well-shaped, though not large, but is gracefully poised on a superb neck. A large and straight rather than a prominent nose; blue gray penetrating eyes which are widely separated and overhung by a heavy brow. His face is long rather than broad, with high round cheek bones, and terminates in a good firm chin. He has a clear though rather colorless pale skin which burns with the sun. A pleasing and benevolent though a commanding countenance, dark brown hair which he wears in a cue. His mouth is large and generally firmly closed, but which from time to time discloses some defective teeth. His features are regular and placid with all the muscles of his face under perfect control, though flexible and expressive of deep feeling when moved by emotions. In conversation he looks you full in the face, is deliberate, deferential, and engaging. His demeanor at all times composed and dignified. His movements and gestures are graceful, his walk majestic, and he is a splendid horseman.

George Washington's first meeting with his future wife Martha and her two children, Patsy and Jacky.

In April, Washington moved his family back to Mount Vernon. In 1761, he inherited the plantation (which he had only been renting before). At age 29, with a total of 9,000 acres under his control, Washington was a major Virginia landowner.

Now he began farming with the same steady thoroughness which had made him successful as a surveyor. He purchased the latest books about farming. When he discovered he could not grow the best grade of tobacco at Mount

A romantic depiction of the wedding of George and Martha Washington, which took place on January 6, 1759.

Vernon, and it was ruining his soil, he switched to wheat. He soon saw there was additional profit grinding grain into flour, so he invested in building his own flour mill.

Since Mount Vernon is located on the west bank of the Potomac River, Washington even went into commercial fishing. Mount Vernon became known for the barrels of salted Potomac fish it sold. Washington also experimented with tree grafting to improve his fruit orchards.

He was soon known as an intelligent farmer, a skilled businessman, a popular legislator, a dedicated elder in his church, and a wise leader in his county.

SOCIAL LIFE AT MOUNT VERNON

Fox hunting was a popular social event at Mount Vernon. In fox hunting, packs of special dogs, known as fox-hounds, chased a fox across the countryside followed by gentlemen on horseback. Washington named some of his hounds Mopsey, Rover, Singer, Drunkard, True Love, and Sweetlips. Fox hunting is still a popular sport in the Virginia countryside.

Washington was an excellent horseman. He rode all his life. Thomas Jefferson said of Washington that he was "the best horseman of his age, and the most graceful figure that could be seen on horseback."

George Washington fox hunting with his friend and neighbor George Fairfax.

One of Washington's best friends and neighbors was George Mason, who lived in this handsome brick home called Gunston Hall.

Although young Washington worked hard to make Mount Vernon a productive farm, he also loved dancing with his guests on such occasions as weekend parties. In fact, he attended a dancing school at one point and continued to practice until he was in his late fifties.

Washington's strength was legendary. One folk story says that as a young man he threw a stone to the top of Virginia's Natural Bridge, a 215-foot-high natural rock arch in the Blue Ridge Mountains. One guest at Mount Vernon in 1772 recalls tossing an iron bar on the lawn with some young men when Washington – then 40 years old – strode up and asked to try. His first toss went far beyond any of the others. Washington told the younger men, "When you beat my pitch, young gentlemen, I'll try again."

The good times, however, did not last. In the late 1760s Great Britain began taxing the colonists to help pay for the war debts it had accumulated protecting the colonies during the French and Indian War. As a legislator and leading landowner, Washington was deeply concerned as the anger of the colonists grew through the 1760s and 1770s.

WASHINGTON'S FRIEND

Washington's knowledge of colonial affairs grew throughout this period under the guidance of his friend and neighbor, George Mason. Mason was seven years older than Washington. He disliked politics and frequently refused political offices offered to him. Therefore, outside Virginia, he was not well known. But he was so highly respected in Virginia that his writings would later serve as an important influence on the Declaration of Independence and important sections of the Constitution, such as the Bill of Rights.

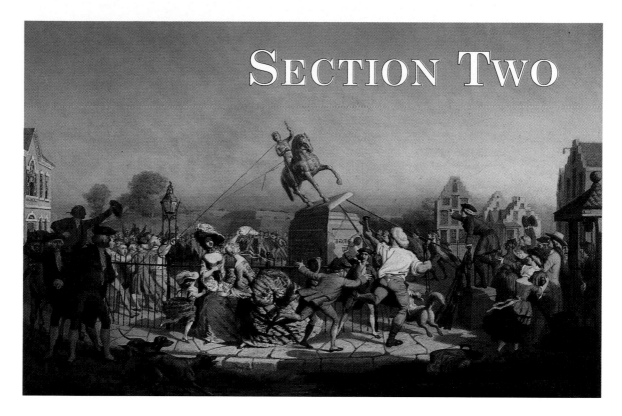

SECTION TWO

THE BEGINNINGS OF THE AMERICAN REVOLUTION

Above, a painting by William Wolcutt depicting the pulling down of the statue of King George III. The statue was later melted down to make bullets for the American army. Courtesy of the Art Gallery, Lafayette College.

In the Revolutionary War, soldiers often stood in a straight line and fired their weapons at the same time, to increase the chances of striking the enemy. Muskets did not have the same accuracy as rifles do today. At left is a formal portrait of King George III of England. How does his clothing differ from the clothing of American leaders?

Chapter 7

Citizens or Subjects?
Causes of the American Revolution

THE COST OF WAR

In 1763, the British Empire was at the height of its power around the world. The combined efforts of the British Army and the American colonial forces had conquered the French and their Indian allies and forced France to give up her colonial hopes in North America. Worldwide, Great Britain had established an empire that circled the globe. British harbors were jammed with shipping and commerce.

But the cost of Britain's victories around the world was high. The British government had borrowed heavily from private bankers, including their own central bank, the Bank of England. The British government's debt was £140,000,000 (£ is the symbol for the British pound, the British unit of money, just like the American dollar is represented by the symbol $). This was a staggering sum for those days. About half of this debt resulted from

One of the stamps that the English required the colonists to purchase as a way of paying taxes.

defending the colonies in North America.

In October 1760, a plump 22-year-old, George III, had become king of Great Britain. He would rule for the next 60 years. One of the King's ministers, George Grenville, Chancellor of the Exchequer (the government official in charge of the Treasury), had a two-step strategy to help pay off the debt:

1. Lower government expenses.

2. Raise taxes.

This plan to help pay off Britain's huge war debt eventually led to the American Revolution. Let's look first at how the British tried to lower its expenses.

PONTIAC'S CONSPIRACY

With the French gone, the American colonists thought they would be able to expand across the continent into the vast, unexplored West. The "West" in 1763 was not what we think of as the West today. It was the land between the Appalachian Mountains and the Mississippi River, especially those areas now covered by the states of Indiana, Ohio, Illinois, Kentucky, and Tennessee.

Already, the areas along the eastern seaboard – from New England to the southern Tidewater – were getting crowded. Land was expensive, and most of it was already owned. For a second or third son, an indentured servant, or those newly arriving with dreams of land ownership, carving out a homestead on the western frontier was their best opportunity for economic freedom.

However, there was still the problem of the Indians. Many of the tribes had already been pushed west, beyond the Appalachian Mountains, and they were unhappy about it. This didn't matter to most colonists. In those days, very few thought of Indians as having the rights as did British citizens.

It did matter to the British government, however. They had made promises to the Indian tribes during the war against the French. The main promise was to keep colonists east of the Appalachian Mountains. But with the disappearance of the French, colonists began to stream westward. Fearful that the settlers would destroy their hunting grounds, in 1763 the Indians went on the warpath. Led by the chief of the Ottawa Indians, Chief Pontiac, the Indians attacked in what became known as Pontiac's Conspiracy. They burned settlers' cabins and killed the occupants, sending colonists fleeing eastward.

CLOSING THE FRONTIER

Now King George III was faced with the prospect of having to keep a British army of 10,000 in the Appalachian Mountains to keep the Indians and the colonists apart. It was too expensive. Great Britain was tired of paying taxes to finance war.

Finally, George III announced that all lands west of the Appalachian Mountains belonged to the British Crown. Known as the Proclamation of 1763, it also ordered all settlers to withdraw temporarily to the east of the crest of the Appalachians. The King hoped the proclamation would prevent the British from having to maintain a large army to keep the peace. In other words, it would lower the cost of governing the newly-acquired lands.

Of course, King George's decree upset many Americans. American fur traders were anxious to pursue the fur trade the French had abandoned. Colonial merchants who had outfitted the fur traders were also angry. Real estate speculators, who had planned to divide up the Ohio valley into small farms and sell the land to settlers, protested as well.

As a result, most Americans simply ignored the Proclamation of 1763. They continued to migrate west, especially into an area known as "Kentucky," led by Daniel Boone and other frontiersmen.

British attempts to stop this flow of colonists westward failed. The Proclamation only succeeded in driving a wedge between Britain and her colonies in North America.

RAISING MONEY

Now let's look at the many ways King George III tried to raise more money to help pay off the British government's debt. Taxes in Britain were already high in 1763 and still going up. Previous British ministers and advisors to the King had avoided the issue of taxing the colonies because it had been so unpopular in the past. But George Grenville insisted that the colonists should help pay part of the debt since at least some of it was due to the cost of defending them from the French and Indians.

So, during the next four years, the British Parliament began passing laws to raise money in the American colonies. Taxes are never popular. But some of these laws caused real financial hardships in the colonies and anger toward the British government as well.

THE SUGAR ACT

The first of these laws was the Sugar Act of 1764. It placed a tax on molasses, sugar, and other products imported into the American colonies from places outside the British Empire. A similar law, called the Molasses Act, had been passed in 1733, but people had not obeyed it for two reasons:
1. The tax was so high.
2. The British government did not try very hard to enforce it.

Any time a government doesn't enforce a law, people start ignoring it. In this case, the colonists openly turned to smuggling – bringing in sugar and

An early example of paper money, printed by Benjamin Franklin in 1760.

molasses secretly to avoid paying the tax. By not enforcing its laws, Britain allowed the colonists to get used to running their own affairs.

But Parliament became determined to enforce the new Sugar Act of 1764. When the British suddenly stiffened enforcement of the law, the colonists resented it. The British used naval patrols and Royal inspectors to search colonial warehouses and even private residences, thus angering the colonists further.

The British even offered a share of the tax to any citizen who reported friends or neighbors who were smuggling. If the person was found guilty, even the police who arrested the smuggler and the judge who found him guilty could receive a large reward. This was a big mistake. It was difficult for someone accused of smuggling to get a fair trial. Many colonists grew deeply angered by this unfair system.

THE CURRENCY ACT OF 1764

Soon after passage of the Sugar Act, Parliament enacted another new law — a law which would plunge the colonies into a financial depression. Business had been expanding quickly in the colonies. Small fortunes were already being made as the colonists began to develop the bountiful eastern half of North America. Shipbuilding was already a big industry. Colonial shipyards were building one-third of all the merchant vessels sailing under the British flag.

To make business easier to pursue, the colonists created their own paper money. It was called Colonial Scrip. It was money issued by colonial governments for the benefit of the people in general. British bankers didn't like this. With the colonies printing their own money, America's economy might soon get out of their control.

To prevent this, the British Parliament passed the Currency Act of 1764. This made Colonial Scrip illegal and forced the colonists to exchange it for British money, issued by the Bank of England. Even worse, the British only gave the colonists one Bank of England note for every two notes of Colonial Scrip. As Benjamin Franklin put it, "The circulating medium of exchange was thus reduced by half."

This was a great bargain for the British. Suddenly, all American products were half price! But Americans had to pay twice the price for all the British products they bought. How would you feel if the value of all your money was suddenly cut in half? You wouldn't think it was fair. It would make you mad at the government which did such a thing. Cutting the money supply of the colonies in half caused tremendous financial problems.

Franklin explained what happened:

> In one year the conditions were so reversed that the era of prosperity ended, and a depression set in, to such an extent that the streets of the Colonies were filled with unemployed.

In fact, Franklin later claimed that the anger caused by this depression was one of the major causes for the Revolutionary War.

THE QUARTERING ACT

The next year, 1765, the British Parliament passed still more inflammatory laws. The first of these, the Quartering Act, made the colonies provide barracks and supplies to house or "quarter" British troops stationed in America. Most Americans believed that the British Army was present just to keep the Americans in line, so the Quartering Act was deeply resented by many.

THE STAMP ACT OF 1765

George Grenville's next action stirred up even more controversy. For years, the British government had taxed her citizens by requiring them to buy government "stamps" for all kinds of official papers. In 1765, Parliament passed a similar law in America which taxed licenses, college diplomas, playing cards, newspapers, advertisements, and legal documents such as deeds to land or mortgages on property – even marriage licenses. The act got its name from the stamp which was put on the documents or materials to show the tax had been paid.

Angry colonists in Boston, Massachusetts, openly burn the Stamp Act declarations to defy King George and British sympathizers.

Americans exploded in anger. Before the law could even take effect, resolutions condemning the Stamp Act poured into Great Britain. Americans had no say in the fairness of this new form of taxation. They had no votes in the British Parliament. All across the American colonies, the new cry "taxation without representation" was heard.

This didn't mean that the colonists wanted to elect their own members of Parliament. Colonial leaders knew that even if they did get to vote there, they would be easily out-voted. Besides, the British Parliament was thousands of miles away. Since telephones had not yet been invented, the only method of communication was sailing ships. How could colonial delegates even know what their constituents wanted?

In the Virginia House of Burgesses, 29-year-old Patrick Henry denounced the Stamp Act in fiery terms. Suggesting that the Act would eventually force the colonies into revolt and be the downfall of King George III, Henry urged his fellow legislators not to turn back: "If this be treason, make the most of it."

Many in the audience gasped in disbelief, including a 17-year-old law student named Thomas Jefferson. According to Jefferson, Henry spoke with "torrents of sublime eloquence" such as he had "never heard from any other man."

Henry's words showed that most Virginians still considered opposition to the Stamp Act as an act of treason. That's because most Americans still felt they were British citizens. But that also meant that they knew British citizens had a long and proud history of struggling with the King to ensure they had a say in the actions of government.

England had undergone a revolution herself only 120 years earlier. King Charles I had struggled with Parliament over the right of the people to have a say in their government. Charles shut down Parliament for 11 years. That caused civil war to break out in England. King Charles lost, not only the war, but also his head at the hands of the victorious leader of the English Civil War, Oliver Cromwell.

When viewed in the light of British history, Patrick Henry's outrage doesn't seem unreasonable. He was merely trying to do what his forefathers had been doing for hundreds of years — give the power to tax to an elected assembly of the people to create a more democratic form of government.

As a result of Henry's famous speech, the Virginia House of Burgesses declared the Stamp Act to be unjust and even illegal. They also passed resolutions that Parliament had no authority to tax Virginians. Throughout the colonies the cry became, "no taxation without representation!"

STAMP ACT CONGRESS

In October of 1765, delegates from nine colonies met in New York. Known as the Stamp Act Congress, they vowed to resist all taxes levied without the consent of their colonial legislatures. Many colonial merchants went a step

Citizens show their defiance by erecting a liberty pole.

further. They vowed to stop importing British goods. Within a few months, products made in Great Britain were harder to buy in colonial stores.

STAMP MASTERS

But the British government pressed on with their plan to squeeze new revenue from the colonies. The King began appointing distributors for the stamps, known as Stamp Masters. But when the Stamp Masters arrived in the colonies, they were often met by angry crowds. Some colonists organized into societies, called the Sons of Liberty. They rioted in the large towns and destroyed the Stamp Masters' offices.

They burned the stamps in public and even applied tar and feathers to the Stamp Masters. Sometimes, they forced them to resign their commissions or sent them running for their lives.

For example, when Stamp Master Zachariah Hood of Maryland refused to resign, the Sons of Liberty destroyed his store and burned him in effigy.

Hood tried to escape to New York on horseback. But he rode the horse so hard it died. He sought safety in a British fort, but when the colonists threatened the garrison, Hood escaped out the back and fled to Long Island. He was finally caught by the determined pursuers and forced to resign his Stamp Master commission.

When the man appointed as Stamp Master for New Hampshire, George Meserve, arrived to take office, he found an angry crowd of patriots waiting for him. Meserve also quickly found it in his best interest to resign. But that wasn't good enough for the Sons of Liberty. They insisted that he burn his commission as well. Meserve later wrote:

> I did not know whether I should have escaped from this mob with my life, as some were for cutting off my head, others for cutting off my ears and sending them home with my commission.

REPEAL OF THE STAMP ACT

The British were shocked at the American defiance. "This is undoubtedly the most serious matter that ever came before Parliament," exclaimed King George III.

British merchants were worried, too. Few in America were buying British products. Many British merchants faced financial ruin. These Britons demanded that Parliament repeal the Stamp Act. They were joined by sympathetic statesmen who had been opposed to the Stamp Act from the beginning. William Pitt, a member of Parliament who later became prime minister, declared, "I rejoice that America has resisted."

In March of 1766, Parliament finally backed down, repealed the Stamp Act and forced George Grenville to resign. News of the repeal caused celebrations throughout the colonies. In New York City, the Sons of Liberty erected a huge flagpole, which they called a liberty pole, and pledged their devotion to the cause of liberty. America had won her first victory over the British.

To the British, the Stamp Act was simply a good decision for increasing revenues. For the colonists, it was an unreasonable demand by a distant government which didn't care about the opinions or economic welfare of its people.

Before the British tried to raise taxes in the colonies, most of the people living in North America loved King George III. They were proud to be citizens of a great empire they were helping to build. The average citizen in Massachusetts or Virginia would proudly say he or she was "a citizen of the British Colonies in North America."

But the actions taken by the British after 1763 showed the American colonists that they were not citizens — they were subjects of the British crown. A citizen is a member of the society by his or her own free will, who has a voice in creating laws which are fair and just. A subject has no control over what laws are enacted. The person is "subjected" to laws or decisions over which he or she has no control. The difference between a citizen and a subject is the

At right, Patrick Henry makes his celebrated speech to the members of the Virginia House of Burgesses. One of the most famous phrases in American history is Henry's emotional argument, "Give me liberty or give me death!"

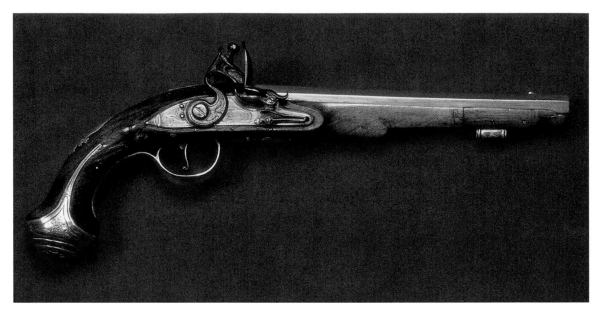

An 18th-century firearm from the Mount Vernon collection.

degree of freedom they enjoy in making decisions about how their government will work. Eventually that difference caused a revolution.

THE TOWNSHEND ACTS

By 1766, Charles Townshend had become the new Chancellor of the Exchequer. Townshend was still determined to make the colonies in America pay their portion of the still huge British war debt. But Parliament was worried that any form of direct taxation, such as the Stamp Act, would lead to more rebellion. So they returned to indirect taxation — taxes which were less visible to the average person — such as taxes on imported goods.

In 1767, Parliament passed several new taxes on all sorts of goods Americans were importing, including glass, tea, coffee, paper, and paint. These were called the Townshend Acts. Parliament hoped that the new taxes would not cause any trouble, since Americans had always paid these sorts of taxes in the past without too much complaint.

WRITS OF ASSISTANCE

And they probably would have, except for the fact that the Townshend Acts also put something new into a controversial enforcement policy known as "writs of assistance." This policy authorized a British official to search any American's business, warehouse, or even home at any time, to look for smuggled goods. This made Americans angry. Attorney James Otis condemned the policy in fiery language:

What a scene does this open. Every man, prompted by revenge, ill humor, or wantonness to inspect the inside of his neighbor's house, may get a writ of assistance.

66

Today, Americans are protected from this form of unreasonable search by the Fourth Amendment to the Constitution. This amendment says that a person's house cannot be entered and searched unless the police go before a judge and get permission to search. The police must present reasonable evidence that laws are being broken and specify for what they are searching.

COLONIAL LEGISLATURES DISSOLVED

The colonies showed their resentment toward the hated writs of assistance in different ways. In New York, citizens refused to obey the Quartering Act. They no longer provided living quarters for British troops. Parliament responded by suspending the colonial legislature. This was the same mistake that England's King Charles I had made in 1629 when he suspended Parliament. Then, it led to the English Civil War and ended in the arrest and execution of Charles.

In Massachusetts, the colonial legislature, led by Samuel Adams, adopted a letter in 1767 urging the other colonies to unite and resist British rule. Parliament responded quickly by dissolving their assembly. Suddenly, every colonial legislature felt it necessary to debate the Massachusetts letter to show support. The legislatures of Maryland, South Carolina, and Georgia promptly adopted the measure. Parliament retaliated by dissolving those legislatures, also.

The colonists were frustrated by the numerous laws and regulations issued by King George.

By overreacting, the British forced the colonists to join together in closer cooperation than ever before. This cooperation was the exact opposite effect the British had wanted.

Americans remembered that refusing to buy British goods had gotten Great Britain to repeal the Stamp Act. They reasoned it might just work this time, too. So they signed agreements to boycott British goods again.

But others took more direct action. Some attacked British customs houses where import taxes were collected. They tarred and feathered anyone who dared to inform on smugglers. Sometimes, even British soldiers were attacked. The British were clearly losing control of America.

Clyde O. DeLand

The engraving above, by Paul Revere, of the Boston Massacre on March 5, 1770, exaggerated the number of Bostonians killed. In the legend it stated that seven died, when only five did. Also, the British Redcoats were surrounded by an angry mob throwing rocks and ice. Revere showed the British commander ordering his men to fire. In fact, they fired despite orders not to do so. The British soldiers were tried for the deaths. Two were found guilty and they received only light sentences. This engraving was designed to fire up the colonists, pushing them closer to a full-fledged revolution. Courtesy of the National Gallery of Art. *At left, a painting by Clyde De Land of the members of the First Continental Congress leaving Carpenter's Hall in Philadelphia in 1774. George Washington, Patrick Henry and Richard Henry Lee were among the leaders at the meeting.*

Chapter 8

Violence Erupts

In October 1768, the British made a foolish decision that had tragic results. They moved over 4,000 troops from Ireland and Nova Scotia to Boston. This transfer was said to be a cost-cutting measure, but many Americans didn't believe that. Only a few years before, Britain had tried to find ways to reduce the number of troops stationed in the colonies. People also wondered why they were all stationed in Boston. Did it have anything to do with putting down the rebellious Massachusetts legislature? Boston was gaining a reputation as a hotbed of trouble-makers. Perhaps the British thought a few thousand troops would keep the Sons of Liberty quiet.

Whatever their intent, the British plan backfired. In Boston, crowds subjected the soldiers to abuse from the moment they arrived. They were called names like "lobster back" or "bloody back" because of their red coats. Children threw stones and snowballs at them. The colonists looked down on the British soldiers because they generally came from the poorer, less educated segment of the British population. Tensions were raised even further because the soldiers were allowed to work at civilian jobs during their time off. This put them in competition with the colonists for jobs.

THE BOSTON MASSACRE

These growing tensions in the colonies erupted into violence in Boston on the afternoon of March 5, 1770. A lone British sentry outside the Boston Custom House became the target of some children's taunts and snowballs. When he called for help, other soldiers joined him. Then they all became the targets of a growing crowd of people throwing snowballs.

One historical account suggests that a man who was half-Indian and half-black, named Crispus Attucks, tried to rally the crowd to take bolder action. When Attucks tried to grab one of the soldier's muskets, it went off in the struggle, killing Attucks. Suddenly, the other soldiers began firing into the crowd, probably fearing for their lives. When the smoke had cleared, four other Boston citizens also lay dead.

The city went wild with anger. The affair was dubbed a "massacre," and the people demanded that the British withdraw all troops from the city. Later, when passions had cooled, the soldiers were tried for murder. They were defended by Josiah Quincy, Jr. and John Adams. Adams would later become the second president of the United States. Neither of these men had any sympathy for the British, but both insisted that every person was entitled to a fair trial. Only two of the soldiers were found guilty, but even those two weren't convicted of murder.

TOWNSHEND ACTS REPEALED

Later in 1770, the new British Prime Minister, Lord North, moved to quiet tensions by getting Parliament to repeal all the Townshend Acts except for the tax on tea. There were good economic reasons for doing this. The Townshend Acts had backfired. Instead of producing extra revenue, they had crippled many British merchants and encouraged colonists to develop their own industries or develop smuggling routes.

That same year, Parliament also allowed the Quartering Act to expire. This reduced tensions between Britain and the American colonies further.

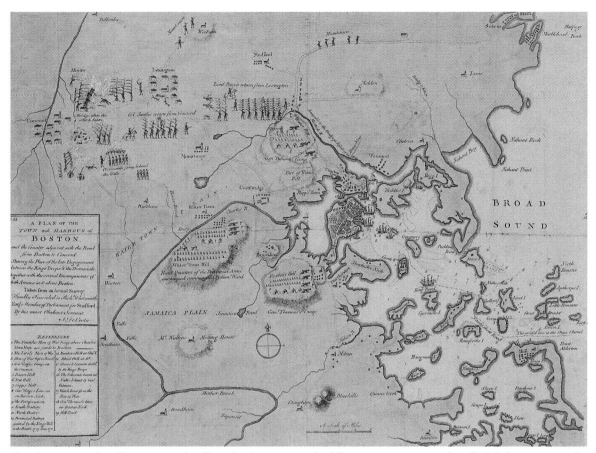

In the events leading up to the Revolution, control of Boston was central to British strategy. In 1775, British and Continental forces clashed at Lexington and Concord.

However, many Americans continued to distrust the British.

Even though the Townshend Acts had been repealed, British customs collectors continued to enforce the older taxes with vigor. Many of these customs officials were dishonest. They took bribes or stole some of the money they collected. This dishonesty continued to anger the colonists, despite the honest efforts of Lord North to restore peaceful relations between Britain and America.

The smoldering resentment Americans felt about British taxes on imported goods flamed to life again in June 1772. Several boatloads of men attacked and burned the British revenue ship *Gaspee* near Providence, Rhode Island. The colonists were upset when the British government announced that the suspected persons would be sent to Great Britain for trial. Why was that upsetting? Because they would be taken far from their homes, probably have to live in a jail cell until their trial, and be away from their families for many months, even if they were not guilty.

At the same time, the British announced in Massachusetts that the

Governor and the judges of Massachusetts would be paid by the British. This would make them more independent of the Massachusetts legislature. If you are paying someone's salary, you have a certain amount of control over that person.

COMMITTEES OF CORRESPONDENCE

In 1772, Samuel Adams, one of the leaders of the Massachusetts Sons of Liberty, had encouraged the colonies to remain organized against the British. He set up a series of committees to communicate information about problems with British policies throughout Massachusetts. These were called the Committees of Correspondence.

These committees became so successful that other colonies soon did the same thing. The colonists quickly discovered that regular communications served an important function in keeping track of British actions in America. Many of the most prominent leaders in the colonies served on these committees. In Virginia, for example, the committee included Thomas Jefferson, Richard Henry Lee, and Patrick Henry.

THE TEA ACT OF 1773

The period of relative calm after the Boston Massacre ended when Parliament passed the Tea Act of 1773. This act actually lowered the price of tea to the colonists. However, the effect of the act was unexpected. The act set in motion a chain of events which would soon lead to open revolt.

When the Townshend Acts were repealed in 1770, an import tax was kept on tea as a way to remind the colonists that Parliament continued to believe in its authority to make laws affecting the colonies, and specifically to tax them. As King George had put it, there must "always be one tax to keep up the right." What he meant was that without some form of taxation, the British would lose control forever.

By 1773, the British East India Company was nearly bankrupt. That company had been started in order to grow and export tea from another British colony, India. But they had been much more successful at growing tea than selling it. By 1773, the company had over 18 million pounds of tea on their hands, looking for a place to get rid of it.

Parliament thought that if it made East Indian tea less expensive, it would sell more of it. Therefore, the Tea Act changed the tax laws by letting the East India Company ship its tea directly to the colonies through its own agents, bypassing American distributors. The British hoped the cost of tea to the average American would go down and consumption would go up.

This act angered colonial merchants who had been making a good living from importing tea, either legally or by smuggling it past British customs officials. Other merchants joined in the protest. If Britain could grant a monopoly on all tea sold in America to the East India Company, it could grant others. As one American merchant wrote:

Would not the opening of an East India House in America encourage all the great companies in Great Britain to do the same?

Merchants stirred up colonial radicals by claiming the Tea Act of 1773 was just another sneaky way for the British to tax tea. But the common man needed little prompting to distrust the British.

THE BOSTON TEA PARTY

Crowds rioted in colonial streets. In Annapolis, a tea ship was burned. Other tea ships arriving in New York and Philadelphia were turned around without even being unloaded.

In Boston, the royal governor, Thomas Hutchinson, was determined to have the ships unloaded and would not let them leave. But the colonists refused to unload the tea. On the night of December 16, 1773, a group of colonists disguised as Indians boarded the tea ships in Boston harbor and dumped their cargoes overboard, destroying 10,000 pounds of tea.

MOTHER OF THE BOSTON TEA PARTY

Sarah Bradlee Fulton and her husband John Fulton were visiting her brother Nathaniel Bradlee and his wife, Ann, at their home near Boston in 1773. John and Nathaniel were asked to join a group of patriots for a raid at

Colonists dressed as Indians dumped 10,000 pounds of tea overboard into Boston Harbor to defy the British on December 16, 1773.

the docks of Boston harbor. Mrs. Bradlee and Mrs. Fulton made Indian clothes for their husbands. They put "warpaint" made from gravy on their faces to make them look like Mohawk Indians.

On the night of December 16, 1773, the group of men boarded British tea ships and dumped 342 casks of tea into the water.

When the men returned, their wives removed the stains from their faces and hid the costumes. For this, Sarah Fulton became known as the "Mother of the Boston Tea Party."

THE INTOLERABLE ACTS

British reaction to what colonists called the Boston Tea Party was swift and cruel. In 1774, Parliament quickly passed a series of laws that Americans called the Intolerable Acts.

The new laws required the port of Boston be closed until the city paid the East India Company for the lost tea. This was a tremendous hardship for a colony that was so dependent upon foreign trade and fishing for its economic well-being.

In addition, the colonial government was restructured. The colonists were granted even less say in how they were governed. One-half of the Massachusetts Assembly, the upper house, was no longer to be elected by the people but was to be appointed by the King instead. Only one town meeting would be allowed each year. Royal officials charged with offenses would be tried in Britain, where they were likely to be found innocent. Finally, the British commander in Boston was allowed to house his troops wherever he saw fit. This new Quartering Act was far worse than the old one. Troops could be housed in private residences against the will of their owners.

FIRST CONTINENTAL CONGRESS

Samuel Adams' Committees of Correspondence were now put to the test. How unified were the colonies? Would they stand together against British tyranny? That summer, a call for a new congress circulated among the colonial committees. In September 1774, delegates from across the colonies met in Philadelphia to decide on a common course of action. This gathering was later called the First Continental Congress.

All colonies were represented except Georgia, and her legislature sent word that it would support whatever action was taken. Among the delegates were George Washington, Samuel Adams, John Adams, and Patrick Henry. Some delegates, like Samuel Adams, were ready to break away from Great Britain immediately. But many of the delegates remained completely loyal to the King. They believed the colonies should obey the laws without protesting. Still others tried to think of ways to persuade the British government to compromise. They still hoped that the King would listen to their pleas, even if Parliament would not. But they were to be disappointed.

The delegates to the First Continental Congress sent a petition to King George III, asking him to intervene on their behalf. In the petition, they asserted their rights to "life, liberty and property." Although they rejected Parliament's authority over them, they still vowed loyalty to the King.

WASHINGTON'S ROLE

The delegates were split generally into two camps – the Patriots, who favored a break with Great Britain, and the Loyalists, who remained loyal to the King. George Washington favored the Patriot group. After being elected as one of the seven delegates from Virginia, Washington wrote, "Shall we...sit and see one province after another fall a prey to despotism?"

In Philadelphia, Washington, now 42 years old, had his first chance to meet and talk with colonial leaders. They were impressed with his sound judgment and military experience. As usual, Washington said very little. He made no speeches. But he worked hard to see that trade with Great Britain was stopped in all the colonies until the Intolerable Acts were repealed.

In the end, Congress agreed to meet again the following spring of 1775 to take further steps if the Parliament had not withdrawn the Intolerable Acts. Throughout the winter of 1774-1775, however, both sides held to their positions. Parliament refused to repeal the Intolerable Acts until the colonists paid for the tea they had destroyed. The colonists refused to pay until the Intolerable Acts were repealed.

CONCLUSION

In many ways, the events leading up to the American Revolution were based on mistakes and overreaction by both sides. But it would be unfair to say simply that both sides were equally at fault. After all, the American colonists believed that as citizens of the British Empire they should have all the rights and privileges granted by the British constitution.

For example, the British Parliament had long ago rejected the power of the King to tax the people without their consent or the consent of their elected representatives. Americans wanted that right, too. They rejected Parliament's right to tax them without the consent of America's colonial assemblies. "No taxation without representation," became a rallying cry for many Americans.

Another factor that fueled anti-British feelings in the colonies was that many colonists weren't English at all, but German, Scotch-Irish, French, or Dutch. They had come to America to start a new life – to be free.

Even many of those who were of English descent considered British society and politics as morally corrupt. Puritan religious ideas supported this view. To them, the actions of the British Parliament in 1763 and after seemed to confirm their beliefs. When open warfare finally erupted between Britain and her American colonies, the American soldiers believed they were defending their rights as British subjects from a Parliament which had gone mad.

The British had been wise enough to create the world's greatest empire. If they had given the American colonies more freedom and reacted more fairly and with less anger during disputes, they might have been able to keep the colonies.

This is the rural road between Concord and Lexington, where Minutemen ambushed the exhausted British troops as they marched back to Boston. At left is the steeple from the Old North Church in Boston, where two lanterns were lit to signal that the British would be "arriving by sea" across the Charles River.

Chapter 9

The War Starts

APRIL 21, 1770,
WILLIAMSBURG, VIRGINIA

Jed, now 29, stood straight and tall at the head of his militia company. The trouble in Boston had brought out the citizen-soldiers. The cruelty of the Townshend Acts and the Quartering Acts had been bad enough. But the shooting of unarmed civilians by British soldiers was too much to bear. Even though the British Prime Minister, Lord North, had repealed most of the taxes, Virginians were still enraged.

Jed had just been promoted by the members of his company. As the new sergeant, he would lead his men during the parade to show local support for the citizens of Boston.

The company captain handed him a halberd, an axe mounted on a long staff, a ceremonial weapon which showed his rank and position. As the drummer began his beat, four boys playing fifes struck up a spirited marching tune. Jed proudly stepped out, leading his company through the streets of Williamsburg.

The crowd cheered as the troops passed, marching in straight, even rows toward the Capitol building a few blocks away. Each soldier looked straight ahead until the company arrived at the foot of the Capitol. "At ease," Jed ordered his men. The soldiers scanned the crowd for their relatives while fiery Patrick Henry gave a short but rousing speech encouraging every Virginian to support the militia.

Afterwards, the artillery men wheeled their shiny bronze cannon into position. While Jed's infantry stood at attention, the artillery fired a volley. When the Captain dismissed the company, Jed looked for his family. He finally spotted his wife, Becky, their four-year-old daughter, Patience, and year-old son, Michael. They were standing in the front yard of William Baker, Jed's old friend from Stanley Hundred. William was a lawyer now, and lived right on Duke of Gloucester Street, the most prestigious street in Williamsburg. Jed hurried over. William reached out to shake his hand.

"The troops looked mighty fine today, Jed," he grinned, "and the company sergeant was especially well turned-out."

Jed looked a little embarrassed as everyone laughed. "It's hot in this getup. Has anybody got anything cool to drink?"

"I've got cider for everyone," replied William's wife, Libby. "Come on inside where it's cooler." Seeing Becky struggling to hold baby Michael, she motioned to a black serving girl of about fourteen. "You can give the baby to Selma." Selma took Michael from Becky and carried him into the house.

Becky gave a sigh of relief. "Thank you, Libby. I love holding him, but after a while he gets pretty heavy."

Jed took some coins from his pocket and handed them to William's daughter. "Frances, you and Patience run into the store there and get yourself some cookies as a treat. Here's a penny for you both."

The girls took the money eagerly and ran away giggling.

A few minutes later, Jed and William sat in the front room of the house with their glasses of cider and some sweet biscuits. "Well, Bill, what do you think of the trouble in Boston? Will the repeal of the taxes quiet things down?"

William Baker looked troubled. "I think Lord North is trying to do the best he can for us in America, but the colonies are very unstable right now. The massacre in Boston came at a very bad time." William passed Jed more cider. "You know, in some ways, Jed, I think the British taxes showed us how little we need England. We're our own country now. I know several hotheads who would like to break our ties, but personally, I think that's going too far."

"So do I," nodded Jed. "I'm glad to know you feel the same way. I can't imagine Virginia prospering without the King behind us. I hope we've seen the last of any trouble between the colonies and the mother country."

"Agreed. But that tax on tea still makes me mad," sighed William. "And I don't like having so many Redcoats over here. That's what caused the killings in Boston. If the British army wasn't so arrogant, it wouldn't have happened in the first place."

"At least they're not forcing us to let soldiers live in our houses anymore," Jed reminded him. William nodded. "Yes, that's true."

Becky appeared at the door. "Jed, we need to get back to the farm soon. Do you want me to have the team brought up?"

William got to his feet. "Don't bother, Becky. I'll send Joseph to get your wagon."

A few minutes later, Jed carried his sleeping daughter from the house and laid her head on a folded blanket. Michael was asleep in his mother's arms. After Jed helped Becky up onto the seat of the wagon, he urged the horses into action with a small tap of the reins.

Jed smiled at Becky. "I'm glad we stopped in at the Bakers', and I still feel the same way about the King."

"I'm so glad you're not trying to stir up trouble like some of the others," answered Becky. "The militia is important, I guess, but I'd hate to see you actually go off to fight the King's soldiers."

"I think the militia is our best way to prevent fighting. If we show the British we're strong, they'll back off and treat us with more respect."

The last rays of the sun were streaking orange in the western sky as the horses turned the wagon onto the lane which led to their farm.

PATRICK HENRY

On March 23, 1775, delegates from every county in Virginia met at St. John's Church in Richmond to discuss the situation with the British. They were also there to elect delegates to the coming Second Continental Congress. They did not meet in Virginia's capital, Williamsburg, however, because they feared that the British Governor of Virginia at that time, Lord Dunmore, might arrest them and ship them back to England where they would face trial as traitors. So they met 50 miles inland. Everyone knew that the British would send reinforcements to Boston and more fighting would take place.

Patrick Henry

79

Still there were those who opposed a complete break with Great Britain.

Patrick Henry, aged 38, disagreed. Henry knew that the British would eventually be able to overwhelm the Massachusetts patriots unless other colonies helped them. In what became one of the most famous speeches in American history, he presented resolutions for equipping the Virginia militia to go to the aid of Massachusetts. Both 43-year-old George Washington and 31-year-old Thomas Jefferson were thrilled by Henry's fiery speech. It ended with the following plea for action:

> Gentlemen may cry peace, peace. But there is no peace. The war is actually begun! The next gale that sweeps from the north will bring to our ears the clash of resounding arms! Our brethren are already in the field! Why stand we here idle? What is it that gentlemen wish? What would they have? Is life so dear, or peace so sweet, as to be purchased at the price of chains and slavery?

Henry's attitude was that of a condemned galley slave. His back was bent as though under the weight of his approaching death. After a solemn pause, he raised his eyes slowly up toward Heaven. Before his stunned audience, Henry held up his crossed wrists, bound by imaginary chains nearly visible. Then, he slowly prayed in words rising to a fever pitch. Henry bent his body backward, his chained hands raised over his head. Every muscle and tendon strained.

> Forbid it, Almighty God! I know not what course others may take...

Henry clenched his right fist as though holding a dagger pointed at his heart. As he drove the imaginary dagger into his chest, he thundered triumphantly:

> ...but as for me, give me liberty or give me death!

As he spoke the word "liberty," his imaginary chains were broken. His arms hurled apart, his hands open. He stood erect and defiant, his face radiant. He paused while the sound of the word "liberty" echoed throughout the church.

As one witness later reported, "His attitude made him appear a magnificent incarnation of Freedom." Another listener was so overcome by Henry's powerful speech that he exclaimed, "Let me be buried on this spot!"

The resolutions passed, and Henry was appointed commander of the Virginia forces. The next year, 1776, he would became Virginia's first elected governor.

LEXINGTON AND CONCORD

Throughout the winter of 1774-75, the colonists had waited to see if the British would withdraw the Intolerable

The Lexington green was the site of one of the war's earliest skirmishes. Captain John Parker and his 80 men were no match for the British troops, who killed eight Americans.

Acts and unblock Boston harbor. Many had believed the British would back down. But with Henry's resolution in Virginia, an increasing number of colonists came to believe that war was inevitable and continued to train local militias and stockpile arms. As one traveler to Virginia wrote in his diary:

> Dined at Colonel Harrison's. Nothing talked of but the blockade of Boston Harbor. The people...talk as if they were determined to dispute the matter with the sword."

Even King George foresaw war with the colonies:

> The New England governments are in a state of rebellion. Blows must decide whether they are to be subject to this country or independent.

The King told the British commander in Boston, General Thomas Gage, to teach the colonies a lesson. General Gage had heard that the New Englanders were collecting guns and ammunition. So he sent out spies into the surrounding countryside to find out the truth. One of those spies was Private John Howe. Howe had been stationed in Boston long enough to learn how Yankees talked and even how they thought. He blended in with the common folk around Boston with ease.

"The King is openly cursed," Howe reported back to General Gage. He told him that the rebellious colonists – now called Patriots – were no longer hoping for a peaceful settlement with Great Britain. The Yankees were ready to fight. They were seen everywhere cleaning guns and drilling openly on village greens. Lists in taverns were posted of those few who still remained loyal to the King. In some places, Loyalists had even been tarred and feathered, and some had their houses burned just because they had dared to defend the British point of view.

But Private Howe had learned another very important piece of information. He had discovered the location of a colonial weapons depot at Concord, Massachusetts, a few miles northwest of Boston.

General Gage decided to move. On the evening of April 18, 1775, soldiers from the British Army in Boston began boarding small boats. They were going to cross the Charles River to raid the colonial arms depot. But General Gage could not hide his troops' movements any better than the colonists could hide their activities from the British spies. The patriots in Boston were watching the British closely. It was to be a fateful night in American history.

PAUL REVERE'S MIDNIGHT RIDE

As the British troops crossed the Charles River, two Patriots waited to sound the alarm. Paul Revere, a silversmith by day, had waited throughout the night. His job was to watch the steeple of the Old North Church in Boston. If the British decided to take the longer route by land, then one lamp would be lit in the church tower. If they tried the shorter route across the Charles River, then the signal would be two lanterns shining from the church tower. Two miles to the south, a fellow Patriot, William "Billy" Dawes, Jr., was looking at the same church tower.

That night, as the British crossed the Charles River, two lamps suddenly appeared in the church tower. The two patriots, Revere from north of Boston, and Dawes from south of town, took off to warn the colonists that the British were headed toward the arms depot at Concord. Soon they were joined by a third man, Samuel Prescott. Of the three men, only Prescott would make it all the way to Concord. The other two were captured en route. Throughout the night they rode, pounding on farmhouse doors along the way, shouting their alarm: "The Redcoats are coming! The Redcoats are coming!"

As oil lamps were lit in kitchens along their routes, worried wives hastily prepared food while their menfolk quickly pulled on their clothes and grabbed their muskets and powder horns. Soon, they set off to join their neighbors at prearranged meeting

Paul Revere will always be remembered for his famous ride to warn citizens that the British were arriving across the Charles River to attack the arms depot at Concord.

places to oppose the British. These were the "Minutemen," members of the militia who had promised to be ready for action at a minute's notice.

LEXINGTON: THE FIRST CLASH

The British troops reached Lexington, about ten miles from Boston, around dawn on April 19. There they were met by the Lexington militia commanded by Captain John Parker. Parker drew his eighty men up in a ragged line, right in the center of Lexington's village green. But he soon saw that he was outnumbered by nearly nine-to-one.

The British commander ordered Parker and his minutemen to lay down their arms. Parker realized that to resist against such a large number of soldiers would be useless. He ordered his men to disperse but refused to have them lay down their arms. No one is sure who fired the first shot, but shortly after Parker had given his order, a shot rang out. Soon, the British line was pouring fire into Parker's men.

A few of the militia did try to return fire, but the British light infantry soon scattered them from the field. As the smoke cleared, eight Americans lay dead on Lexington's green, and another nine had been wounded.

ON TO CONCORD

Following the fighting, British officers moved their men back into column formation and continued the march toward Concord. Before they could reach the quiet Massachusetts village, however, the townspeople had moved the powder stores to safety and gathered their militia for yet another attempt at stopping the British. Word of the skirmish at Lexington had spread rapidly ahead of the British. Outside Concord, militia units from all over New England gathered. Over four hundred men turned out to oppose the British.

British soldiers entered Concord unopposed but found little there of military significance. They burned a few

Paper was a fairly valuable commodity in the 18th century because it was made by hand, often one sheet at a time.

gun carriages but conducted themselves properly toward the townspeople. To the militia outside the town, however, the smoke rising from among the distant houses made it look like the British were burning the town. The commanders ordered their men forward in an effort to stop the British and give townspeople a chance to put out the fires.

At the north bridge outside of Concord, the two sides finally came face to face with one another. For the British, their mission was already complete. All their officers wanted to do was withdraw their soldiers to Boston. The New Englanders had other ideas.

Unlike Lexington, there was no question about who fired the first shots. Here, British soldiers fired first.

"My God, they are firing ball!" screamed the startled commander. He thought the British would only fire just to scare the Americans, with no actual bullets in their muskets.

"Fire for God's sake – Fire!" he shouted again. In an instant, both ends of the bridge disappeared in clouds of gun smoke as the militia returned fire and held their ground. Three British soldiers and two Americans died in the exchange.

The British commanders quickly decided to retreat. They began to withdraw to Boston, a long sixteen miles away. For a mile or two, everything was peaceful, then suddenly the woods on either side of the road exploded in musket fire.

Militia units that had arrived too late to help their friends at Lexington

The British forces opened fire on the Patriot Minutemen as they crossed the bridge outside Concord. Three British soldiers and two Americans died.

and Concord were able to position themselves along the tree-lined road to Boston where they could ambush the British as they marched. A fourteen-mile, running battle developed. British light infantry tried to keep the woods clear of the militia, but the British soldiers had been marching and fighting nearly twenty-four hours and were exhausted. The militia, however, were fresh. Only the arrival of British reinforcements saved what was left of the original British force.

Compared to other battles that followed, the engagements at Lexington and Concord were only small skirmishes. Yet they were vitally important to the American Revolution. Only 146 Americans were killed or wounded compared to the loss of 264 British soldiers. That evening, as the British soldiers hobbled back into Boston, the curious citizens saw bloody bandages and men in tattered uniforms. The American victory encouraged the colonists. From villages and farms across New England, militia units marched toward Boston bent on driving the British army into the sea. That night, the hills around the city twinkled with hundreds of campfires built by thousands of Patriots from the surrounding countryside.

The significance of the battle was that Britain and America were no

longer talking about their differences. Shots had been fired and lives lost. Although the Americans had not yet declared their independence, the Revolutionary War had begun.

FORT TICONDEROGA SEIZED

Within three weeks of the Battle of Lexington and Concord, another colonial force struck the British far to the west. Patriots under the joint command of Benedict Arnold and Ethan Allen captured British-held Fort Ticonderoga and Fort Crown Point on Lake Champlain.

On the night of May 9, 1775, Ethan Allen, with sword in hand, led his men to the gangway of Fort Ticonderoga. Known as the "Green Mountain Boys," because they were volunteers from the Green Mountains of what is now Vermont, Allen and his men surprised the guard and forced their way into the fort. Yelling at the top of his lungs, Allen ordered the commander and his garrison to surrender. The British were so surprised that they gave up without a fight.

With the capture of that great fortress, Americans gained a large number of powerful cannons which they dragged over the mountains to Boston. But the Americans still lacked the strength and the organization to attack. The British, on the other hand, found themselves unable to leave except by sea. Both sides watched and waited.

Because America possessed no organized army with established officers and formal training in the early days of the war, men from all walks of life put down their tools and picked up their muskets to support the cause. Men like blacksmiths were particularly valuable to the Revolutionary forces, because they could create the tools, horseshoes and wagon parts that were vital to the war effort. At left, Ethan Allen demands the surrender of the British commander at Fort Ticonderoga.

BOSTON

CHARLES TOWN

At the Battle of Bunker's Hill in 1775 (above), British ships ferry troops across the Charles River from Boston. They burned Charlestown and then attacked the Americans on Breed's Hill. At left, a map of Boston showing the establishment of both British and American camps about a year later when George Washington and his troops forced the British to evacuate the city on March 17, 1776.

Chapter 10

The Siege of Boston

SECOND CONTINENTAL CONGRESS: MAY 10, 1775

Shortly after the outbreak of fighting at Lexington and Concord, delegates to the Continental Congress began the trip back to Philadelphia. They had agreed to meet again in the spring of 1775 to discuss the situation concerning the British. With the British troops in Boston totally surrounded, the delegates met on May 10, 1775 in Philadelphia, the day after the Green Mountain Boys captured Fort Ticonderoga.

Some of the delegates, such as Samuel Adams of Massachusetts and Patrick Henry of Virginia, were ready to declare independence right away. Their plan was to seize British officials and ask France and Spain for help. George Washington had for many years thought war with Britain was unavoidable. In fact, he wore a military uniform to the Second Continental Congress to show his willingness to fight if necessary. But he was probably still hesitant to break with Britain at this time, and the majority of the colonists agreed that they still wanted to avoid war.

Those wanting to remain British won out. Led by John Dickinson of Pennsylvania, they wrote the king that they had "not raised armies with ambitious designs of separating from Great Britain." But they also coupled a plea for peace with a stern message. If the British continued to use force, the Americans would resist with force. To show they meant business, they appointed George Washington to command the Continental Army. Washington had military experience and, by appointing him, a Virginian, the northern colonies hoped to persuade the southern colonies to join in more enthusiastically.

Washington had not sought the position. The Congress voted him a monthly pay of $500, but Washington turned it down. He said he would keep track of his expenses and would ask only for reimbursement. Washington accepted his new position as commander in chief of the Continental Army with typical modesty. He told the Congress:

I beg it may be remembered by every gentleman in the room that I...do not think myself equal to the command I am honored with.

BATTLE OF BUNKER'S HILL

Now the Patriots surrounding Boston were an army – the Continental Army. But before Washington could travel to take his new command in Cambridge, Massachusetts, just across the river from Boston, fighting broke out again.

General Gage, the British commander, was desperate to break out of the Boston peninsula. In June the Americans pushed their defensive positions closer to Boston along the Charlestown peninsula north of Boston. The Americans learned that the British were planning to try to break out by occupying some of the hills around Boston. To prevent this breakout attempt, on June 16, 1775, American commanders were ordered to fortify Bunker's Hill on a small peninsula overlooking Boston from the north. But they made a mistake. In the middle of the night, they dug their trenches on a smaller hill known as Breed's Hill, which was much closer to the waterfront.

General Gage was quick to decide that this was the opportunity to teach the Americans a lesson. He ordered the British General William Howe to storm the position the next day. The British began their attack by lining up 2,500 soldiers and marching up the hill in straight rows towards the 1,600 Americans dug in on Breed's Hill. The American soldiers had very little ammunition. They had to make every shot count and their muskets had a very limited range. They were told to wait until the British were very close before opening fire. Word was passed: "Don't fire until you can see the whites of their eyes."

As the British soldiers approached, the only sounds heard were those of officers barking orders against a background of drums and marching men. Behind their defenses, American soldiers watched and waited. Then, when the British were less than 50 yards away, the order was issued – "Fire!" The musket balls tore great holes in the British line, and the Redcoats staggered back in confusion.

But the British officers reformed their lines and proceeded forward again. For a second time the Americans waited until the British closed to less than 50 yards. Another volley tore into the British ranks, and more Redcoats toppled. Again, the British retreated.

There was much excitement among the Americans, even though they were almost out of ammunition. It looked like the British might give up. The Americans knew that one more attack would exhaust their ammunition supply. Finally, much to their dismay, the Americans saw General Howe order his Redcoats to line up for a third attack. The Americans fired a half-hearted volley at the attackers and then fell back, using their muskets as clubs.

The British were able to chase the Americans back up the peninsula. Although considered a defeat for the Americans, the cost to the British Army was high. The British had lost 226 men killed with another 828 wounded. The Americans lost only 145 men dead with

another 304 wounded. One American General, Nathanael Greene, said, "I wish we could sell them another hill at the same price." Of course, the mothers of the slain did not agree.

Although the Americans lost the Battle of Breed's or Bunker's Hill, they again saw the weaknesses of the British Army's way of fighting – marching into battle in straight, even rows. They began to believe the British could be easily defeated and that there was no need to build a permanent professional army. Both ideas would be proven wrong in the coming years of war.

Shortly after the American defeat, the Second Continental Congress, still meeting in Philadelphia, took further steps to strengthen its position. It sent ambassadors to several European countries, including France, Spain, and the Netherlands, to request aid.

Back in Great Britain, King George III was shocked. He felt the Battle of Bunker's Hill had been a great disaster for the British. He immediately clamped a tight naval blockade on all the colonies. This blockade was to prevent shipping from reaching the colonies with supplies. The King also proclaimed that all the colonists were rebels. Now there was no turning back.

WASHINGTON ARRIVES AT CAMBRIDGE

In July 1775, 43-year-old George Washington arrived in the Boston area to take command of the American army. By now, over 14,000 men had gathered from all over New England outside Boston. Washington was disappointed to see that most of the troops were badly equipped and undisciplined. The men were in need of food, clothing, and shelter.

Washington soon began to bring discipline to the ragtag fighting force. But he was still deeply troubled about their ability to fight the British Army. He wrote: "The fate of unborn millions will now depend upon God and the courage and Conduct of this Army."

Washington did not immediately order an attack on the British. One of the reasons was that his new army still lacked big guns and ammunition. Fortunately, the British didn't realize how poorly supplied the new Continental Army was. Had the British attacked that summer, each American soldier would have had only enough powder to fire nine shots.

THE CANADIAN EXPEDITION

Late in 1775, the Second Continental Congress sent a military force into Canada to encourage French-Canadians to rise up against the British. They thought that a Canadian rebellion would weaken the British by forcing them to defend themselves on a second front. They hoped opening a second front would force the British to withdraw from Boston. Unfortunately, the French-Canadians did not want to get involved.

The expedition into Canada was led by Richard Montgomery and Benedict Arnold. The Americans captured Montreal on November 13. But, attacking Quebec later, under cover of a blinding snowstorm, they were beaten back. Montgomery was killed, and Arnold was severely wounded. Despite the defeat, Arnold was promoted to Brigadier General.

Although the Americans maintained the siege of Quebec through the winter, the arrival of British reinforcements in the spring forced the Americans to retreat back to Fort Ticonderoga in New York.

THE BRITISH GIVE UP BOSTON

The siege of Boston lasted throughout the fall and winter of 1775 and into 1776. The Americans strengthened their position by moving to Boston the cannons captured from the British at Fort Ticonderoga. They pulled them on sleds over the snow, through nearly 200 miles of the forests of New York and Massachusetts.

In early 1776, Washington occupied Dorchester Heights overlooking Boston. His artillery chief, Henry Knox, could then use the cannons to shell the hundreds of British ships sitting in Boston Harbor. That surprise move caught the British napping. They awoke one morning to see their own cannons looking down on them from Dorchester Heights.

Sir William Howe, who had replaced General Gage as the British commander, decided it was impossible to hold the city. On March 17, 1776, the British fleet lifted anchor and sailed to the safety of Canada. With the fleet

Probably the most famous painting of the Battle of Bunker's Hill is this one by Jonathan Trumbull of the death of Dr. Joseph Warren, a prominent Boston physician (in light blue).

went the entire British Army and about a thousand Americans who remained loyal to the King. For the first time in years, the colonies were free of British soldiers. But soon, the British would regroup and land on Long Island, near New York City; later they would try to take the southern harbor at Charleston, South Carolina.

The Americans had still not given official notice that they intended to be independent. Many people, even some in the American army, hoped that the fighting would end quickly and a peaceful solution could be found. But for other colonists there was no turning back. Nothing but independence would satisfy them. In just a few weeks in Philadelphia, Thomas Jefferson would begin work on the document that would proclaim America's independence to the world – the Declaration of Independence.

The Second Continental Congress met for weeks in Philadelphia and finally decided to appoint a committee of five men charged with writing the Declaration of Independence. At left is Benjamin Franklin, one of the most respected, creative and powerful leaders in 18th-century America.

Chapter 11

Independence Declared

In Philadelphia, the debate over independence raged at the Second Continental Congress for weeks. Those opposed to a complete break from Great Britain argued against independence for at least three good reasons:

1. The stability of the British system of law and order was a prize the British had fought and died to achieve. Giving up that precious system in hopes of getting something better had to be carefully considered by thoughtful people.

2. As long as the colonists were merely resisting certain unfair acts of Parliament, they could count on powerful friends in Great Britain. But they knew the British would unite to fight to preserve the British Empire if independence were declared.

3. Last but not least, if the colonists revolted and then lost the war, the British might declare them to be traitors and after the war have them executed.

Richard Henry Lee

Those who favored independence had four good arguments for a break from Great Britain:

1. The colonists had already shed blood in defense of their rights.
2. If Patriot soldiers were captured by British troops, as citizens of an independent nation, they might be treated as prisoners of war under British law, instead of being shot as rebels.
3. The Continental Congress could take away the property of all citizens who remained loyal to the British.
4. The Patriots would have a better chance of winning the help of the French or the Spanish by claiming independence from the British

Empire. In other words, anything that weakened the British Empire was good for Spain and France.

On June 7, 1776, Richard Henry Lee from Virginia introduced a resolution to Congress declaring "these United Colonies are, and of right ought to be, free and independent states." Four days later, before voting on Lee's resolution, Congress appointed a committee of five men to rewrite the declaration.

These men were:

- **Benjamin Franklin**, Pennsylvania, age 70
- **Thomas Jefferson** Virginia, age 33
- **John Adams** Massachusetts, age 40
- **Robert Livingston** New York, age 29
- **Roger Sherman** Connecticut, age 55

Who were these five men? Let's take a closer look.

BENJAMIN FRANKLIN (1706-1790)

Benjamin Franklin was born in Boston, the tenth son of 17 children. His father was a soap and candle maker. He went to school only until he was age 10. But Franklin believed that "the doors of wisdom are never shut." Eventually he would master the basic principles of most of the sciences and

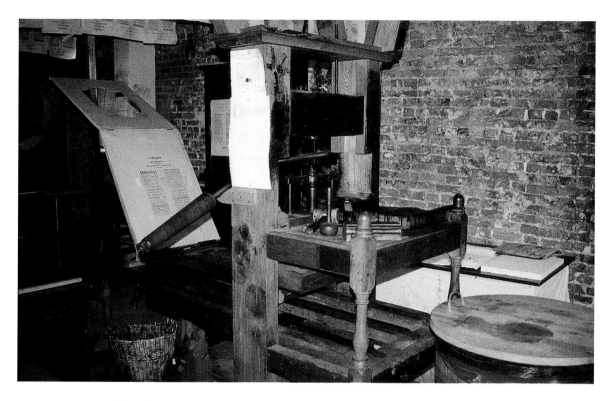

Franklin Press at Franklin Court, Philadelphia, Pennsylvania.

study five foreign languages.

At 12, he started working for his brother as a printer. But the brothers argued frequently. At age 17, Franklin went off on his own. He traveled to Philadelphia, the largest city in the colonies.

When Franklin was a young man, he, like his soon-to-be friend, George Washington, was very interested in encouraging goodness with good advice. He drew up a list of thirteen virtues he wished to acquire. He also outlined a program for practicing them in his *Autobiography*. "I was surpriz'd to find myself so much fuller of Faults than I had imagined, but I had the Satisfaction of seeing them diminish," he wrote.

In 1729, Franklin became the printer of the paper money of Pennsylvania. At the same time he began publishing a colonial newspaper, the *Pennsylvania Gazette*, and *Poor Richard's Almanack*. The *Almanack* was filled with humor and proverbs praising honesty and hard work. For example, Franklin wrote, "Early to bed, early to rise, makes a man healthy, wealthy, and wise." He helped establish the first fire department, the first lending library, and a school which eventually became the University of Pennsylvania.

In 1748, Franklin gave up managing his publications and devoted himself to his interest in science. He was one of the first to experiment with electricity. In 1752, he flew a kite in a thunderstorm to demonstrate that lightning was really electricity. As a result of his findings, he invented the lightning rod. When lightning hit Franklin's home, his own lightning rod saved it, proving Franklin's remark that "An ounce of prevention is worth a pound of cure."

Franklin was the first scientist to study the movement of the Gulf Stream in the Atlantic Ocean. He proposed daylight-saving time in the summer, saying it was wasteful for people to "live much by candle-light and sleep by sunshine." He invented bifocal eyeglasses – a reading lens and a distance lens set in the same frame.

Franklin popularized the game of chess in North America by writing a book on its educational value. He also invented an instrument called an "armonica," or glass harmonica. It used glasses filled with different levels of water that were normally played by rubbing the tops of the glasses with moistened fingertips. The armonica was a mechanical version. It became so popular that the famous composer Mozart wrote two pieces of music for it.

In 1753 Franklin took the position of deputy postmaster general for all the colonies and made many improvements. Twice between 1757 and 1775 Franklin lived in London, where he became the unofficial ambassador for the colonies. After the Revolution, Franklin served as a delegate to the Constitutional Convention at the age of 81.

Benjamin Franklin also invented the "armonica" or glass harmonica, which was once a very popular musical instrument. Now, it is estimated that only 10 people in the world are accomplished players of the glass harmonica, including this performer, Dean Shostock.

THOMAS JEFFERSON (1743-1826)

Thomas Jefferson was born near Charlottesville, Virginia, the third of eleven children. His father, Peter, had served as a surveyor, sheriff, and member of the Virginia House of Burgesses.

He started his schooling at age nine. At that time, he was sent to live with a nearby Scottish clergyman who taught him Latin, Greek, and French. Jefferson's father died when he was only 14. As the oldest son, he inherited the family farm, Shadwell, with its 30 slaves and more than 2,500 acres.

At age 16, Jefferson entered the College of William and Mary in Williamsburg. Through his college professors, Jefferson met the British governor of Virginia, Francis Fauquier. He spent many evenings at the governor's mansion and later commented that, "to the habitual conversation on these occasions I owed much instruction."

Although reared in the Anglican Church, Jefferson developed a distrust of organized religion. His religious views were an important influence on American life and are still being felt today. Long after the Revolution, Jefferson would be credited with the notion that church and state should be separated. It is interesting to note that Jefferson at first admired Patrick Henry, but later they became bitter enemies.

After writing the Declaration of Independence, Jefferson resigned from Congress and returned to the Virginia legislature. Although he had called for

Thomas Jefferson

strong military action, he had no interest in serving in the military himself. He did not fight in the Revolutionary War.

In 1794, after five years in office as the nation's first Secretary of State, Jefferson persuaded Washington to let him resign and return to his home, Monticello. In 1800 he opposed John Adams in the presidential election and won. Jefferson thus became the third U.S. president.

JOHN ADAMS (1735-1826)

John Adams was born near Boston. He became a lawyer and a teacher of law. Although in 1770 he helped defend the British soldiers who participated in the Boston Massacre, he had spoken out forcefully against the Stamp Act five years earlier. Later, he and his cousin, Sam Adams, were among the first colonial leaders to insist that the American colonies should seek independence from Great Britain. He helped persuade Congress to organize the Continental Army. He also pushed for George Washington's appointment as the leader of that army.

When Richard Henry Lee presented his resolution that the colonies should be free from England, John Adams seconded the resolution. He was probably the hardest-working member of the Second Continental Congress.

Adams would become the first vice president of the United States and then the second president. His appearance was quite different from George Washington's. Where Washington was tall, Adams was short and stout. But there were other differences as well. Where Washington was well loved for his quiet modesty, Adams was never as popular. He admitted to being blunt and impatient. But, like Benjamin Franklin, Adams had a good sense of humor. He was the first president to live in the White House and the only one whose son also became president.

Adams and Jefferson had bitter differences of opinion after the Revolution. Later, through correspondence, they became friends again and both died on the same day, July 4, 1826, exactly 50 years after the Declaration of Independence was signed.

ROBERT LIVINGSTON (1746-1813)

Robert Livingston was born to a wealthy family in New York City. As a young lawyer, he was devoted to the cause of liberty. He worked on numerous committees of the Continental Congress at Philadelphia, especially in the areas of finance and foreign affairs.

In 1777 he became the first governor of New York (then called Chancellor). Four years later, he became the first head of what would later be called the State Department. When George Washington was sworn in as the first president in 1789 under the new Constitution, Robert Livingston administered the oath of office.

John Adams

ROGER SHERMAN (1721-1793)

Roger Sherman was born near Boston, Massachusetts. He was a lawyer and served as a judge in Connecticut for many years.

At first, Sherman feared that the Patriots would go too far, but he was one of the first to claim that the British Parliament had no power over the colonies.

Sherman was very influential during the Constitutional Convention of 1787. It was he who presented the compromise which resolved the differences between the large and the small states and allowed the U.S. Constitution to come into being. That agreement gave us our two houses of Congress, the House of Representatives and the Senate.

DECLARATION OF INDEPENDENCE

Jefferson was asked by the other four men to do the actual writing of the Declaration of Independence. After Franklin and Adams made changes to Jefferson's first draft, the committee presented the Declaration of Independence to Congress on June 28, 1776. But Congress didn't discuss Jefferson's document first. They returned to Richard Henry Lee's resolution. On July 2, they adopted Lee's resolution, officially declaring the new United States of America to be independent of Great Britain.

Then Congress turned to Jefferson's Declaration. After making several more changes, the completed Declaration of Independence was adopted on July 4, 1776. That's why we celebrate the 4th of July as Independence Day. John Hancock, the president of the Congress, signed the document first in large letters. He said he wanted to be sure King George could read his writing without his glasses.

JOHN HANCOCK (1737-1793)

John Hancock was adopted by an uncle after his father died. His uncle, Thomas Hancock, was the wealthiest merchant in Boston.

When John was 27, his uncle died, and John inherited his business. Four years later, an incident on one of Hancock's merchant ships caused the British to move over 4,000 troops from Ireland and Nova Scotia to Boston.

John Hancock

Hancock's ship arrived in Boston harbor carrying a cargo of wine. When the British customs officer came on board to collect the tax on the wine, the crew locked him in a cabin and unloaded the wine without paying the tax.

The British seized the ship and took Hancock to court. When a series of riots broke out, the British decided to send in massive reinforcements.

Hancock became known to the British as one of the most dangerous rebels. He worked closely with Sam Adams for independence. In fact, both were in Lexington in 1775 when British soldiers marched on that town. Had it not been for the midnight ride of Paul Revere, both would have been arrested.

Hancock wanted to be appointed commander in chief of the Continental Army, despite being five years younger than George Washington and lacking military experience. He was disappointed that Congress chose Washington.

At age 39, Hancock was president of the Second Continental Congress when it ratified the Declaration of Independence in 1776.

THE PREAMBLE OF THE DECLARATION

The Declaration of Independence has become one of history's most cherished documents. In it Congress appealed to the people of both Europe and America for their support. The first part, called the Preamble, states the purpose of the document. It says, in part:

When in the Course of human events, it becomes necessary for one people to dissolve the political bands which have connected them with another ... [then] they should declare the causes which impel them to the separation.

NEW THEORY OF GOVERNMENT

Next, the Declaration of Independence states a new theory of government with these famous words:

We hold these truths to be self-evident, that all men are created equal, that they are endowed by their Creator with certain unalienable Rights, that among these are Life, Liberty, and the pursuit of Happiness.

Unalienable rights are rights which cannot be taken away. It would be many years before slaves and Native Americans would be granted liberty, but at least this was a start. When Jefferson talked about "the pursuit of happiness," that marked a significant change in colonial thinking. For many years, one of the sayings leading up to the revolution had been, "life, liberty, property." Jefferson had replaced the word "property" with the words "pursuit of happiness." Owning things is not a right, but having the opportunity to succeed is.

The Declaration goes on to state:

Whenever any Form of Government becomes destructive

of these ends, it is the Right of the People to alter or to abolish it, and to institute new Government...

In other words, if government interferes with these unalienable rights, then the people have the right to change the government.

A DECLARATION OF FREEDOM

In a brief conclusion, the Declaration states that the colonies have the right to be free and independent states and that the political connection between them and Great Britain is "totally dissolved." In the final sentence, all the signers declare that they are relying on God's protection. The signers also agreed to support their cause with everything they had, saying, "We mutually pledge to each other our Lives, our Fortunes, and our sacred Honor."

JULY 4, 1776

Jed's daughter, Patience, was sweating, but she was happy with her work. She and their slave, Sarah, were helping make soap for next year's use.

Sarah and her husband, Ezekiel, had been purchased by Jed Warwick more than a year ago to work on the farm. Sarah and Ezekiel had a boy named Tom. He was just the age of Michael, Patience's brother. Although Michael was only five then, he and Patience had helped Sarah and Ezekiel fix up one of the run-down slave huts

The wash house at Mount Vernon was a very busy place, where the smell of soap was always present.

behind the outdoor kitchen.

Patience especially liked Sarah. Although she was a bit younger than her own mother, Sarah knew so much. She had a home remedy for practically every ailment. And she knew lots of stories. Just then, she was telling a story about how a rabbit outwitted a farmer in the corn patch. Patience listened intently as she watched Sarah cut up the fat for the soap.

Soap making was an annual summer task. All year long, the Warwick family kept a large covered crock in the outdoor kitchen into which they threw any scraps of fat, meat trimmings, used lard, rancid butter, and so forth. Then on a summer day, they would throw the animal fats into a pot of boiling water to "wash" away the impurities. In another operation, they would pour water through wood ashes to make what is known as a hot "lye" solution. They would then boil the lye solution down until it would begin to thicken just a bit.

"Mama always said to boil it 'til an egg would float in the water," said grandfather Warwick.

Then the animal fats were added to the lye solution and the mixture was boiled until it thickened some more.

Next, the mixture was strained and poured into a large crock. Now it would be used as we use liquid soap from a bottle today.

Soap making was a smelly process. Patience found it almost magical, however, that such a nasty mess turned into the soap that kept the people and their clothes and floors clean all year long, even if it did smell a little like smoky ashes.

Patience and her mother, Rebecca, were carrying the fatty pieces to the cast iron pot as Sarah cut them up. Then her mother measured the other ingredients into the pot.

"Patience, you need to keep the pot stirred up until we're finished," cautioned her mother. "I know it's a hot job, but it won't take all day. We'll be through by lunch time."

Grandmother Warwick had died the previous spring. Patience's grandfather, Tom Warwick, had been sickly through the winter and had come to live with them at the beginning of the summer. He had hired a couple to run the mill because his son, Jed was fighting in General Washington's army.

Grandfather had the rest of the menfolk planting fruit trees behind the barn.

"Patience, we'll finish the soap," said her mother. "You get a basket and pick us new beans for lunch."

Patience enjoyed working in the garden. As she picked the beans, she thought about her father, off with the army in New York, far away. She worried about him a lot. So did mother. But they prayed for him every day asking that God would protect and guide him.

As she stuck the pitchfork under a leafy potato plant she thought of how good it felt to be ten. She was a big girl now. No longer one of the little kids. She was excited that her uncle and aunt were coming from Williamsburg with her cousins to celebrate her birthday.

About three o'clock, mother took Patience and Michael inside for a nap to avoid the hottest part of the day. Later, as the shadows lengthened, Patience and her mother made mint tea with cool spring water.

Suddenly Patience heard the sound of horses. She ran into the yard. Yes, it was her cousins. They were standing in the wagon bed as her uncle pulled the horse to a stop. Soon, the girls were sitting under a shade tree making dolls out of dried corn husks. The boys were off wading in the creek while the grownups sipped mint tea in the parlor.

That night, the three girls all crawled into Patience's bed. They talked and giggled long after Patience's mother was quiet. Even the girls knew that history was being made in Philadelphia. It was history that would not only change their lives but also the way all people would look at government from then on.

SECTION THREE

THE WAR OF INDEPENDENCE

The Battle of Princeton proved to be a clear victory for the Americans, providing an emotional lift to Washington and his soldiers.

As the war progressed, Washington's army became more and more organized and experienced. At left, a portrait of the General by Charles Willson Peale.

Chapter 12

The War: 1776-1777

After the British were chased from Boston in March of 1776, no British soldiers could be found anywhere in the thirteen colonies. This, as Washington suspected, was merely the calm before the storm.

The commander of the British army, General William Howe, was busy devising a plan to retake the rebellious colonies. The first step was to seize a major American port city in the north, as well as one in the south. George

Washington thought he knew where the British would strike next. While the Second Continental Congress was debating whether to declare independence, Washington began moving his army from Boston down to New York.

Why was Washington so sure the British would attack New York? Because New York City had an excellent harbor and sat at the mouth of the Hudson River, the largest river in the colonies. The city would not be easy to defend. General Howe could land his soldiers at more places than Washington could cover.

BATTLE OF MOORE'S CREEK BRIDGE

The British also had plans to conquer the southern colonies, hoping to rouse loyalist support for the crown in North Carolina. With the expectation of thousands of British troops being sent to help, loyalists formed a force of 1,500, including many immigrants from Scotland, part of the British Isles. The little army moved toward Wilmington on the coast of North Carolina to join up with a large British fleet being sent from New York.

But Colonel James Moore of the American forces learned of the loyalist plan. He successfully moved troops to hinder their march to the coast. On February 27, 1776, the two forces opposed each other across the banks of Moore's Creek near Wilmington. Americans had removed planks from a bridge, but the fierce Scots attacked

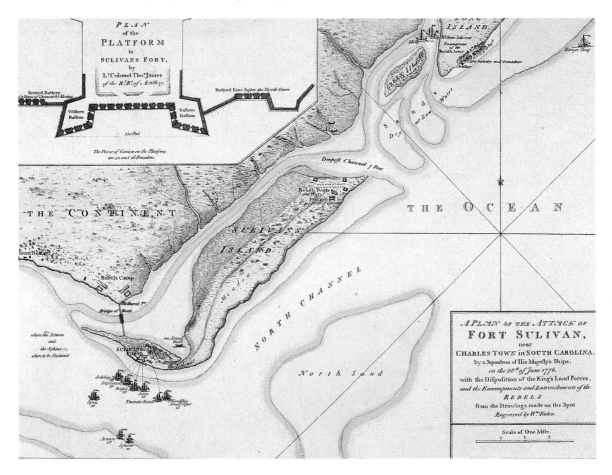

This British map shows their plan to attack Fort Sullivan near Charles Town, South Carolina in June 1776.

anyway over slippery logs, waving their huge traditional swords, called claymores, in the frosty morning mist. Waiting on the opposite bank, American militia cut down the tottering Scotsmen with deadly musket and cannon fire. Those loyalists not shot down into the cold deep waters began to retreat, losing many prisoners and much equipment. This little battle has been called "the Lexington and Concord of the South," because it ignited patriot fervor in North Carolina.

BATTLE OF SULLIVAN'S ISLAND

The British made their next move in the summer of 1776. A powerful British army was dropped off on Staten Island across from New York City, while a fleet of over 50 vessels set sail southward for Charleston, South Carolina. It carried several thousand British soldiers.

On the morning of June 28, 1776, the day the Declaration of Independence was presented to Congress in Philadelphia, the British fleet attacked. Only a small garrison of colonists guarded the approach to Charleston's harbor. Their fortress, on Sullivan's Island, is now known as Fort Moultrie to honor the heroic commander at that time, General William Moultrie.

In Charleston, a few miles across the harbor, concerned residents gathered on balconies, rooftops and even church steeples that warm summer morning to watch the battle. Ten British warships opened fire on Fort Moultrie with a total of 318 cannon. The tiny fort, manned by only 344 Continental soldiers and a few militia, responded bravely with only 30 cannon and a number of South Carolina's best sharpshooters.

One advantage the colonists had that the British hadn't counted on was that Fort Moultrie was constructed of spongy palmetto logs which tended to absorb the impact of the British cannon balls. The British also put 2,000 army regulars ashore on an adjacent island in order to attack the fort by land. The British troops had to cross by small boats to reach Sullivan's Island, and Fort Moultrie was manned by some of South Carolina's best marksmen. Although several attempts were made by the British Army, the marksmen were able to turn them back with heavy losses each time. Eventually the British were forced to abandon this plan altogether.

As night fell, after 10 hours of nearly constant cannon fire, the British fleet withdrew. The cost to the British was frightful. The little fort's cannon had taken a deadly toll. Every man stationed on the quarterdecks of every British ship at the beginning of the battle had been killed or wounded. The whole loss to the British was 255 killed and wounded, while the patriots inside Fort Moultrie lost only 10 dead and 22 wounded.

The shattered British fleet retreated all the way back to New York. It was the first time the Americans had encountered a regular British fleet. Like the Battle of Moore's Creek Bridge

This 1858 illustration from the magazine Harper's Weekly *shows the Americans at Sullivan's Island firing on the British fleet. The sand and palmetto-log fort absorbed the British shelling while the British ships took a terrible pounding and eventually withdrew.*

in North Carolina, it was a decisive American victory, and a humiliating experience for the British. Six days after the Battle of Charleston, the Declaration of Independence was signed.

THE BATTLE FOR NEW YORK CITY

In August 1776, American soldiers watching the approaches to New York harbor saw the next phase in the British plan unfold as the horizon filled with the masts of British ships. The British fleet numbered over 30 warships and 400 troop transports. General William Howe, the British commander at Bunker's Hill, was in command. His brother, Admiral Lord Richard Howe, who headed the British Navy, joined him in the battle for New York.

On board the transports were 32,000 soldiers, over 8,000 of whom were mercenaries from an area of present-day Germany known as Hesse. These Hessian soldiers were hired out to the British by Prince William of Hesse-Kassel, one of the many monarchs in Europe.

This army was the largest armed force Britain had ever sent to the New World. Washington, by contrast, could only muster 14,000 soldiers, many of them from relatively untrained militia units.

The New York campaign proved to be a disaster for the Americans. General Howe beat Washington at nearly every turn. But Howe never was able to catch Washington. Washington was forced to learn how to retreat quickly out of harm's way. Howe had outmaneuvered the Americans on Long Island and on August 27 forced them to retreat across the East River to Manhattan in small boats under the cover of darkness and fog. Had Howe cut off Washington's escape, the war might have ended then and there.

General Howe invaded Manhattan on September 15, 1776. After another series of defeats, Washington's army was chased southwest across the Hudson River and into New Jersey.

Washington reached the Delaware River ahead of Howe. After taking time to sweep the eastern shore to destroy any boats that Howe might use to follow him into Pennsylvania, he crossed the river to safety.

Thinking the American army was now beaten, Howe left smaller parts of

George Washington directing the retreat from Long Island on August 29, 1776, one of the most astonishing and successful retreats in history.

his army, called garrisons, behind in New Jersey, and then withdrew to New York City to spend the winter. Howe's secretary, Ambrose Serle, boasted:

> ...the Heart of the Rebellion is now really over...its dying groans now clear for all to hear.

THE BATTLE OF TRENTON

Things did not look good for Washington. On December 18, he wrote his brother, John Washington, and said that unless something could be done to increase the size of the army and improve its condition, "I think the game will be pretty well up."

Morale was low. Washington realized that his army was about to evaporate. By the end of the year, the enlistments of all but 1,400 soldiers would expire. He knew that most of the men would choose to go home to help their families through the winter rather than stay and fight.

Practically everyone thought that Washington would have to stop for the winter and try to rebuild in the spring. But Washington knew that unless he could do something to rekindle hope in the minds of his soldiers and the American people, there would soon be no army to rebuild. Instead of seeking a safe place to spend the winter, Washington began looking for an opportunity to strike a blow that would breathe new life into the war effort.

It was at this time that a fiery writer named Thomas Paine sounded another call to action in a pamphlet called *The Crisis*. Washington found

Washington took a great risk in leading his men across the icy Delaware River, but the plan succeeded. They caught the Hessian soldiers off guard at Trenton, New Jersey.

The American victory at Trenton was an important one, providing a sense of confidence and enthusiasm to Washington's troops.

Paine's writings so inspiring that he had them read to his entire army:

> These are the times that try men's souls. The summer soldier and the sunshine patriot will, in this crisis, shrink from the service of his country. But he that stands it now deserves the love and thanks of man and woman. Tyranny, like hell, is not easily conquered; yet we have this consolation with us, that the harder the conflict, the more glorious the triumph.

Washington found a suitable target

in the small town of Trenton, New Jersey. General Howe had left only a garrison of Hessian soldiers under the command of Colonel Johann Rall. Washington knew that when winter came, most European armies stopped all but the most necessary activities. He hoped Rall would do the same.

On Christmas night, 1776, Washington set his tiny army back into motion. Boat crews carried the army across the ice-choked Delaware River toward the New Jersey shore. Cold winds drove sleet into the men's faces, adding to their misery and making their muskets useless. Knowing the weather would be bad, Washington had

A rare artifact from the Revolutionary War — George Washington's towel.

ordered his artillery chief, Henry Knox, to bring several big guns along. Foul weather could not easily make cannons useless, as it could muskets.

In Trenton, Rall and his officers had been enjoying Christmas. They had a pleasant meal and a little too much to drink, unaware that George Washington was coming. Once across the river, the Americans began their march to Trenton, just nine miles away.

Washington's army struck from two directions, crushing the Hessian garrison in between. The plan worked perfectly. Rall and his men were caught by surprise. After a weak attempt at resistance, the Hessians surrendered. Rall and 30 of his men were killed. Washington took 981 prisoners and captured much-needed supplies. Giving the British no time to react, Washington quickly moved his army back across the Delaware River to safety.

General Howe rushed troops into the area under General Charles Cornwallis. Washington waited for a few days, but was not ready to stop fighting for the winter. On December 30, the day before many of his men were scheduled to go home, Washington crossed the Delaware again. This was a risky move. Not far from Trenton, the British caught up with Washington. The fire from Knox's artillery was all that kept the British from storming the American position.

That night, the American army slipped away to the north. Washington left a small group of soldiers to keep numerous campfires burning brightly to make the British think they were still there. He was about to strike deep into the British rear to frighten and confuse them.

At Princeton, the Americans ran into two British regiments. This time, the odds were in Washington's favor. His Continental regulars easily threw back the Redcoats and took the town.

1777 - DIVIDE AND CONQUER

The British were now determined to end the war in 1777. In London, Lord George Germain, King George's foreign secretary, devised a simple plan to cut off New England from the rest of the colonies. Once the head of the American Revolution was cut off, he believed, the rest of the colonies would quickly fall. Lord Germain's plan called for three different armies, coming from different directions, to meet in Albany, New York.

- One would move south from Canada along Lake Champlain and take Fort Ticonderoga and Saratoga, New York, before moving into Albany.
- A second smaller force would move eastward from Lake Ontario to the Mohawk River.
- A third force from New York City would move up the Hudson, destroying American positions along the river, and join the other two armies.

There were many problems with this plan. The biggest was the difficulty of coordinating such a complex venture. Of course they had no radios or telephones in those days, so they had to rely on messages sent by couriers on horseback.

From the north, General John Burgoyne started southward from Montreal on June 15, 1777. From the west, Colonel Barry St. Leger headed eastward toward Albany from Lake Ontario in western New York. From the south, General Howe was supposed to march north towards Albany but never did. No one knows what happened to Howe. He may not have gotten the orders in time. It is also possible that he decided he had a better plan than Lord Germain back in London.

To the north, Burgoyne's force of 7,000 made painfully slow progress during the summer. They had to hack their way through the thick forests of upstate New York. To make matters worse, one of Washington's generals, General Philip Schuyler, had succeeded

British General John Burgoyne surrenders to General Horatio Gates, center, as General Daniel Morgan in white buckskins looks on. The surrender took place at Saratoga, New York, on October 17, 1777.

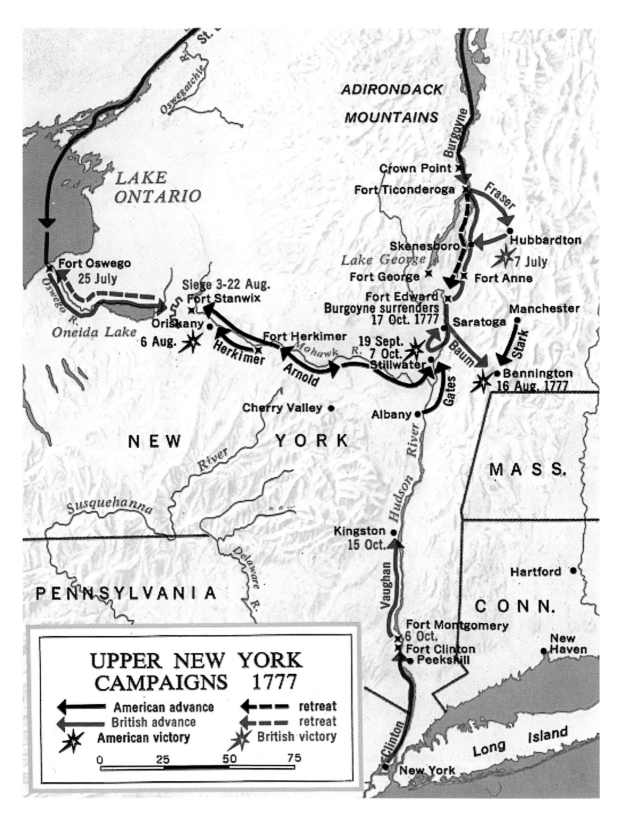

LAKE ONTARIO

ADIRONDACK MOUNTAINS

Crown Point ✗
Fort Ticonderoga ✗

Fraser

Burgoyne

St.

Oswegatchie

Oswego R.

Fort Oswego
25 July

Siege 3-22 Aug.
Fort Stanwix ✗

Oriskany
6 Aug. ✶

Oneida Lake

Herkimer

Fort Herkimer

Mohawk R.

Arnold

Skenesboro
Lake George
Fort George ✗
Fort Anne ✗

Hubbardton
✶ 7 July

Fort Edward ✗
Burgoyne surrenders
17 Oct. 1777

19 Sept.
7 Oct. ✶

Stillwater

Saratoga

Baum

Manchester

Stark

Gates

Bennington
16 Aug. 1777 ✶

Cherry Valley ●

Albany ●

NEW   YORK

MASS.

Susquehanna River

Delaware R.

PENNSYLVANIA

Kingston ●
15 Oct.

Vaughan

Hudson River

Hartford ●

CONN.

Fort Montgomery
6 Oct. ✗
Fort Clinton ✗
Peekskill ●

New
Haven ●

Clinton

Long   Island

New York ●

UPPER NEW YORK
CAMPAIGNS   1777

⟵ American advance   ⟵ retreat
⟵ British advance   ⟵ retreat
✶ American victory   ✶ British victory

0   25   50   75

in gathering sizable numbers of militia in the region. Although not ready to oppose Burgoyne openly, they slowed his progress even further by cutting huge trees to block the trails.

After a series of smaller engagements, an American army under Horatio Gates brought Burgoyne to a stop near the small settlement of Saratoga. Burgoyne's provisions were running low. His supply lines were stretched thin up into Canada. He knew he had to attack.

In a series of battles that came to be known as the Battle of Saratoga, Burgoyne threw his soldiers at the Americans, but they were beaten back by General Benedict Arnold, who fought brilliantly until seriously wounded. Exhausted, Burgoyne surrendered his entire army of nearly 6,000 at Saratoga on October 17, 1777.

To the west, St. Leger wasn't doing any better. He only made it about halfway to Albany. After an unsuccessful attempt to take Fort Schuyler at the head of the Mohawk River valley, he was forced to retreat on August 23.

The offensive that Howe was supposed to mount from New York turned into a halfhearted attempt to rescue Burgoyne. Howe's subordinate, General Henry Clinton, made good progress up the Hudson with a small force. He made it about two-thirds of the way — to Kingston — before receiving news of Burgoyne's surrender. The Germain plan was dead. It was a complete victory for the Continental Army.

The Americans went wild with joy at the news of Burgoyne's defeat, but it was a dark day in London. The British Parliament sent ambassadors to the Continental Congress offering to suspend the Intolerable Acts and pardon the Patriots. The Americans refused their offer. In France, news of the Saratoga victory convinced the French that America had a chance against the British. They began to consider joining the Americans.

THE DEFENSE OF PHILADELPHIA

General Howe had decided to direct his main force against Philadelphia, rather than to go to Albany, believing that the fall of the Patriot capital might bring the war to a close. But instead of marching overland from New York to Philadelphia, Howe put his army back aboard the British fleet and sailed southward. American scouts followed his progress all the way down the coast to the mouth of the Chesapeake Bay. After sailing his fleet up the bay, Howe marched his troops through southern Maryland to attack Philadelphia from the south.

Washington had anticipated this plan. He intercepted Howe at Brandywine Creek on September 11, 1777, but once again Howe defeated the Americans. Washington's forces met the British again on October 4 north of Philadelphia at Germantown, and again they were beaten. Howe captured Philadelphia and settled in for another winter. Washington's forces were forced to fall back to Valley Forge, Pennsylvania, about 20 miles to the west of the city.

These cannon line Artillery Park at Valley Forge, Pennsylvania. At left, a soldier prepares to fire his musket.

Chapter 13

Valley Forge

Washington selected Valley Forge for his encampment because it was close enough to Philadelphia to keep an eye on the British, yet was in the middle of rich farm lands which could feed the army through the winter. Although that winter was not unusually harsh, the Continental Army suffered considerable losses.

The British had already stripped most of the area of food supplies, so the officers responsible for buying food for the army – the commissary officers –

were unable to purchase much of what was left because inflation had made their currency worth very little. The British had also been printing fake Continental currency – known as counterfeiting – and flooding the market with it.

The combined lack of food, shelter and warm clothing led to disease. Many soldiers deserted Washington's army that winter and over 2,500 soldiers perished, more than had died in battle so far. Washington angrily wrote

Washington was respected by his soldiers because he endured the same hardships they did at Valley Forge.

Congress, asking if they believed his troops were "made of sticks and stones, and equally insensible of frost and snow." He told Congress that his men lacked clothing for winter – even shoes – because every day he saw their bloody footprints in the snows of Valley Forge.

On January 6, 1778, the 20-year-old Marquis de Lafayette, a French officer who joined Washington's staff as a volunteer, was horrified over conditions:

> The unfortunate soldiers were in want of everything; they had neither coats nor hats, nor shirts, nor shoes; their feet and legs froze till they grew black

and it was often necessary to amputate them.

FRANCE HELPS AMERICA

While Washington's troops were suffering in Valley Forge, Benjamin Franklin was in Paris trying to convince France to come to America's aid. France had secretly been providing the Americans with desperately needed ammunition and supplies, but Franklin wanted more. His reasoning was that if America lost her war for independence, the British Empire would become stronger and France weaker. Eventually his arguments won out.

In February 1778, France signed

two treaties with America. One was a trade agreement, and in the other France agreed to recognize the independence of the United States of America. Later, in June, France also agreed to wage war on Great Britain until the colonists were free. Both countries agreed not to make a separate peace with Great Britain.

The French treaties came at a good time. Despite the great American victory at Saratoga, the Americans were in bad shape. Washington's army was starving in Valley Forge. But the good news filled the Patriots with new hope. Recruits began to pour back into the Continental Army.

Baron Frederick von Steuben (1730-1794)

In addition to France, both Spain and the Netherlands began sending aid to America. Also, volunteers came from across Europe to help the American army. Baron Frederick von Steuben, a Prussian military officer, joined the Americans in 1778. Prussia (part of present-day Germany) then had the best trained army in the world. Washington had suffered some bitter defeats. He knew that if his troops were to win against the British they would need to be better trained. Soon, the men began training constantly under von Steuben.

Baron von Steuben, however, was not what he had claimed to be. He told Washington that he was a lieutenant general (a three-star general) in the army of Frederick the Great. It turned out that von Steuben had risen only to the rank of captain. Washington was aware of von Steuben's exaggeration but chose to ignore it. The Americans needed him. He was made a general.

Von Steuben proved to be a godsend to the army. He developed a simpler drill that made it easier for the soldiers to learn. Von Steuben's new methods made it possible for officers and sergeants to train their soldiers to the same standards that British soldiers had attained. Von Steuben also drastically reduced the number of motions it took to load and fire the muskets. These improvements would soon begin to pay off. The Continental Army that emerged from Valley Forge in the spring of 1778 was different from the ragged group of men who had set up camp there in December 1777.

March 1, 1778

The guard came to attention and saluted smartly as Jed approached his hut after surveying his units before dawn. Finally, the long, cold night was coming to an end.

The trunk used by George Washington during the Revolutionary War, which is currently on display in the master bedroom at Mount Vernon.

121

The March to Valley Forge, by William B. T. Trego, depicts the cold and desperate conditions Washington's army faced during this difficult period of the war.

"*Good morning, Corporal Smithfield,*" *said Sergeant Major Jed Warwick. "You look a bit chilly. You can go down to the kitchen and get something hot to drink.*"

"*I am that, sir,*" *the young corporal nodded and smiled. "But the night wasn't as cold as a month ago." Then he saluted again, "By your leave, sir," and departed.*

The first rays of the sun brought a warm breeze from the south. "Thank God!" Jed thought, "it looks like we are going to have a spring day after all."

Through the long and awful winter there at Valley Forge, Jed sometimes had wondered whether the Army would survive. Units that should have had 200-300 men had as few as 30-40. Now, with spring approaching, men were joining the army again, and the

ranks would begin to swell with returning soldiers.

But this spring, the army would be better than any which had ever faced the British before. The difference was General von Steuben's training. As soon as he arrived, the daily routine changed. The units began to drill in European styles of movement, learning to change direction and move from marching columns to fighting lines and back in a twinkling of an eye.

Muskets were cleaned and polished daily. Soldiers began bayonet training as well. They learned to fight as skillfully with the sharp bayonets attached to the ends of their muskets as the Redcoats did. No longer would they be afraid to take the enemy on in hand-to-hand combat.

As Jed settled into his hut he

re-read the letter to Becky he'd written the night before.

March 31, 1778, Valley Forge
Dear Becky,

I hope that you are well. We are doing much better here. The bitterest of the winter is over and supplies are arriving daily. Our rations are much improved. But the greatest change in the Army is our training. Never again will we be as afraid as we were last year. We are gaining confidence in ourselves and in one another as each day passes.

We have a spirit of discipline that was not there before. I wish you could see the exactness with which we march and maneuver. I do not think we shall again have difficulty in moving when we are in contact with the King's army. I am almost eager for our first engagement. I feel confident that we shall surprise the enemy on that occasion. Please tell the children I am thinking of them.

Your affectionate Jed Warwick

He folded the paper, melted a little sealing wax, put it where the folded edges came together, addressed the front, and put it in his pocket to mail at the first opportunity.

Baron Friedrich von Steuben drilling newly-trained troops at Valley Forge, Pennsylvania.

MONMOUTH COURTHOUSE

The decision of the French to come to the aid of America was a major turning point in the war. From that point on, the British turned their attention to the southern colonies. There they hoped to enlist the aid of numerous British loyalists, called Tories.

The British commander, General Howe, was replaced by Sir Henry Clinton. Clinton had been ordered to take the British army camped in Philadelphia south to strike at the southern states. But instead of returning to the closest seaport at the top of the Chesapeake Bay, Clinton decided to march them back to New York across New Jersey.

This gave Washington the chance he needed to test his newly-trained army. The Americans gave chase and caught the British army at Monmouth Courthouse, New Jersey on June 28,

1778. Although General Clinton struck back hard, the Americans stood their ground. There was no clear-cut victory that day. Each side lost about 350 men, but the British army fled to New York.

Technically, the battle was a draw. But in reality, it was the first time the American army had stood up to the British army on a European-style battlefield. The Americans had won their share of battles in the past because they had some special advantage, either in position, numbers, or surprise. Without some sort of edge, they had almost always failed to last long against the better-trained British.

Washington felt that "the men must be brought to face danger" in an open battlefield. When the Americans faltered, then began to retreat, Washington rallied them to stand firm. Lafayette dramatically described Washington's fearless leadership that day:

The reconstructed huts at Valley Forge show of the small and simple quarters in which the American soldiers survived.

124

I [Moses Greenleaf Capt. in Col. Tuppers Regt.] do acknowledge the UNITED STATES of AME-RICA to be Free, Independent and Sovereign States, and declare that the people thereof owe no allegiance or obedience to George the Third, King of Great-Britain; and I renounce, refuse and abjure any allegiance or obedience to him; and I do [Swear] that I will, to the utmost of my power, support, maintain and defend the said United States against the said King George the Third, his heirs and successors, and his or their abettors, assistants and adherents, and will serve the said United States in the office of [Captain of a Foot Company] which I now hold, with fidelity, according to the best of my skill and understanding.

Sworn before me in Camp [Moses Greenleaf]
at Valley Forge May 10th 1778
Jno. Paterson B Genl

American soldiers were asked to sign a pledge swearing allegiance to the United States, not to King George III.

...his graceful bearing on horseback, his calm courage ... as he rode all along the lines amid the shouts of the soldiers, cheering them by his voice and example. I thought that never had I beheld so superb a man.

When an officer protested that Americans would not be able to stand up to British regulars, Washington thundered: "Sir, they are able, and by God they shall do it!" And they did.

As darkness fell over the Monmouth battlefield, both sides were exhausted after a full day of fighting in heat that approached 100 degrees. Many men died not of gunshots but of heat stroke. A French volunteer remembered "we slept on the field of battle amongst the dead, whom we had no time to bury."

A heroine of the battle was Mary Hays, known as "Molly Pitcher" because in the midst of the heavy fighting she carried water in pitchers to the terribly thirsty men. When her husband fell wounded, she took his place on an artillery piece and fought bravely alongside the soldiers.

It was a very good day for the Americans. The Battle of Monmouth showed that the Continental Army was at last a professional force.

By the close of the war American soldiers, above and left, were well-disciplined and confident – a very different sort of army than the one that assembled in 1775.

Chapter 14

The Later Years of the War

THE BRITISH TURN SOUTH

The summer of 1778 marked the start of the third year of the war. Despite significant battlefield successes, the British were still in search of a winning strategy. The Americans had not given up. Early in the war, the British strategy was to cut off New England from the rest of America. The surrender of Burgoyne's army at Saratoga had ended that plan.

Howe had hoped that taking Philadelphia would demoralize the Patriot cause. The city had fallen, but the rebellion lived on in spite of the loss. Valley Forge had been critical. The American army should have fallen apart and disbanded. But it didn't. Somehow they survived. Valley Forge had been the lowest point for the American Revolution. Although in their weakened state the Americans didn't realize it, by surviving that long, cold winter in Pennsylvania they had shown the British that they could survive anything. By doing so, they snatched success from what looked like a hopeless situation.

THE IMPORTANCE OF VALLEY FORGE

What the British had failed to understand was that Washington's army was the heart of the rebellion. Despite being chased by the strongest army in the world, which was supported by the world's largest navy, Washington had survived. Every time he was cornered, Washington escaped the British net. As the *Pennsylvania Journal* applauded him in 1777:

> Washington retreats like a general and acts like a hero. Had he lived in the days of idolatry, he [would have]... been worshipped as a god.

Washington's strategy was simple. He would win the war by not losing his army to the British, since he believed that: "the possession of our towns, while we have an army in the field, will avail [the British] nothing.... it is our arms, not defenseless towns, they have to subdue."

Washington's quiet character and solid determination were largely responsible for keeping his army together that winter. He lived with his men. He endured their hardships. He always saw to their comfort first. Putting others first is called self-sacrifice. It was one of Washington's best qualities. The French general, the Marquis de Lafayette, wrote to Washington to encourage him that winter:

> If you were lost for America, there is nobody who could keep the Army and Revolution for six months.

Washington's strategy was simple. He knew that he lacked the manpower or resources to defeat his foe quickly and decisively. Instead, he would make time his ally. The idea was to extend the conflict, making it so costly that it would become unpopular at home in Great Britain. The effectiveness of this hit-and-run strategy of Washington's changed the way wars would be fought in the future. The French alliance, as well as assistance from other European countries, aided Washington's strategy immensely. It added to Britain's costs and complicated her problem of retaking the American colonies.

THE NEW BRITISH STRATEGY

As a result, the British decided to turn to the southern colonies. Two factors drove this unusual strategy. First of all, regaining the thirteen states became a secondary objective, especially after the draw at Monmouth. In other words, Britain had pretty much given up on retaking the northern states held by Washington's army. Also, the entry of France into the war changed the situation considerably. The French fleet now threatened Britain's possessions in the Caribbean.

Moving operations into the southern states would allow the British army and navy to consolidate their forces and still be prepared to defend against the French in the Caribbean.

Secondly, King George III and his advisors had repeatedly heard that large numbers of loyalists still existed in the south. The presence of the British army, King George believed, would bring them out of hiding and rally them to the side of the Redcoats. If they could conquer the southern colonies, then perhaps the British could consider taking the north again later.

From then on, major military activities ended in the north. Although there were a few instances of British raiding parties attacking coastal towns near New York City, and some action in Ohio and as far west as the Mississippi River in what would later become Illinois, the bulk of the British army and navy moved south. The British strategy was to occupy major southern port cities, then have their army sweep inland, plundering and burning in an effort to terrorize the Patriots into submission.

SAVANNAH

The first of these attacks came in December 1778 when the British seized Savannah, Georgia. They also intended further moves in 1779, but found themselves tied down with problems and had to postpone the effort until 1780.

BENEDICT ARNOLD (1741-1801)

The year 1779 was one of relative quiet on the battlefield. One important event, however, was that General Benedict Arnold decided to betray the new nation he had fought for so bravely in the past. He would become America's most famous traitor.

After the Battle of Saratoga, since General Arnold's wounds had left him crippled, George Washington gave him command of Philadelphia. Arnold lived extravagantly and was denounced for violating several state and military regulations. In April of 1779 he married a young society woman who was loyal to the British, Margaret Shippen. Soon after, Arnold made a secret agreement with the British to try to obtain command of an important place and then betray it to the British.

The next year he tried to do just

Benedict Arnold

John Paul Jones

that. He informed the British that he would be given command of the great fortress at West Point, New York. He demanded £20,000 for turning over West Point, and half that sum if he failed. Arnold was exposed in 1780 when a British spy, Major John André, was captured carrying papers General Arnold had sent to the British. Arnold escaped to New York and became a general in the British army. Major André was hanged as a spy.

Arnold later led British expeditions which burned Richmond, Virginia, and New London, Connecticut. He went to England after the war and although he met with King George and was later granted 13,400 acres of land in Canada, he did not find happiness in England. He was not warmly accepted. He died

deeply in debt and without friends.

JOHN PAUL JONES (1747-1792)

Another important event in 1779 was the most famous naval battle in the war, led by Captain John Paul Jones. Often called the father of the American Navy, Jones was a leader whose heroism fighting against larger and better-equipped British ships is legendary.

Jones was born with the name John Paul in 1747 in Scotland. At age 12, he joined the British Navy, and by age 22 he was given command of his own ship. A few years later, he fled to the American colonies when his crew mutinied and he was accused of murder. He probably added Jones to his name to hide his identity.

He joined the Continental navy in 1775 and served on the *Alfred,* the first American ship purchased by the Continental Congress. Jones soon distinguished himself for bravery. In 1778 he raided the Irish coast in the first ship to fly the new American flag, the Stars and Stripes, and soon thereafter captured the British ship the *Drake.*

In 1779 Jones was given command of the *Bonhomme Richard.* It was a French ship, given to the Americans by the French king. Many of its crew were Frenchmen, but it flew the American flag.

On September 23, 1779, Jones met a large British convoy in the North Sea. He boldly attacked the lead warship, the *Serapis,* which was much larger and better equipped.

Jones took his vessel alongside the British ship so that the muzzles of the ships' guns touched and the rigging of their sails became entangled. Jones' ship was so badly damaged that it was about to sink, so he lashed the two ships together and the crews fought in hand-to-hand combat for three hours. At the height of the battle, Jones was asked to surrender. To that he made the defiant statement for which he is best known, "I have not yet begun to fight." Eventually the British surrendered. Jones' ship sank, so he took command of the *Serapis*.

After the war, the United States abolished its navy. Jones wrote on naval tactics and eventually was employed by Russia's Catherine the Great in her naval battle against the Turks. Jones is buried in the chapel of the U.S. Naval Academy at Annapolis, Maryland.

CHARLESTON

Meanwhile, back in the southern colonies, in February and March 1780, General Clinton was ready to try to seize more southern territory. He landed forces outside Charleston, South Carolina, and surrounded a large American army there. Now Charleston was under siege by the British, just as Washington had held Boston under siege in 1775-1776.

On May 12, 1780, with their city under constant bombardment from British guns, the citizens of Charleston convinced the American commander, General Benjamin Lincoln, to surren-

Lord Cornwallis, leader of the British forces at Yorktown.

der. Yielding to their pleas and seeing that further bloodshed would be futile, he surrendered his entire force of 6,000 soldiers. In addition, the British obtained three American warships and 300 cannon in the process. For the Americans, it was a devastating loss. This was nearly the entire American army south of the Potomac River.

CORNWALLIS' MISTAKE

Following the fall of Charleston, Clinton returned to New York, leaving General Charles Cornwallis to finish the job of conquering the south. Had the British taken a more friendly

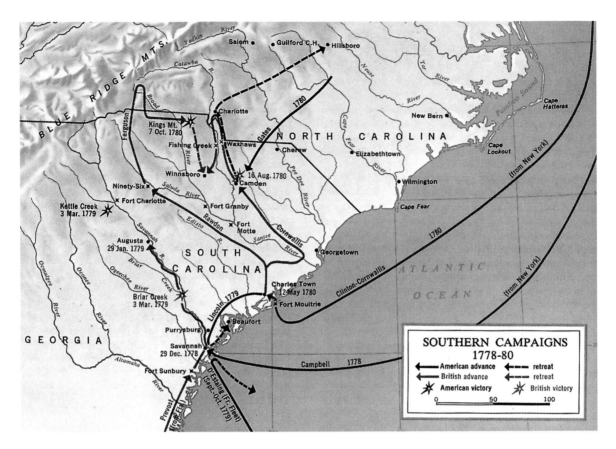

The southern campaign may have proved victorious for the British, but they made the mistake of plundering the countryside, turning all of the colonists into determined patriots.

approach to the people of the Carolinas, the job might have been easy. But instead, now that the British army could go wherever it wanted, the soldiers ran wild, plundering the countryside and hardening the determination of the Southerners to oppose them.

Patriot fighting bands sprang up, led by men such as Francis Marion, the legendary "Swamp Fox." Other leaders such as Thomas Sumter and Andrew Pickens adopted Washington's hit-and-run tactics. They made life miserable for the British by raiding their outposts and ambushing their supply wagons. But Washington, still positioned out-side New York City to threaten the British, knew that these tactics could only keep the British off balance. He needed a general to head up the southern campaign. He had several men in mind, but the Continental Congress overrode his suggestions and sent General Horatio Gates southward with a small army to oppose the British.

Gates was a poor choice to lead the new army. In August 1780, he took his forces to Camden, South Carolina, where Cornwallis crushed them, thanks to Gates' inept handling of his soldiers.

Seeing his army defeated, Gates

fled the field, leaving his soldiers to the mercy of the British. After Gates' defeat, Washington selected a new commander for the south, General Nathanael Greene.

The situation in the south was by now more desperate than ever. Two American armies had been lost, and few reserves existed from which Washington could build a new army. Things were going well for the British in the southern states. In May of 1780, after the fall of Charleston, South Carolina, General Cornwallis had easily overrun the entire state. To make matters worse, Loyalists were enlisting on the side of the British in record numbers.

In September 1780, the British released a prisoner and sent him home to the western Carolinas with the message that if the people there did not quit their opposition, the British army would march "over the mountains, hang their leaders, and lay their country waste with fire and sword." But this threat only angered the settlers to the west.

KINGS MOUNTAIN

In October 1780, a band of frontier settlers known as the "over-mountain men," from what today is the state of Tennessee, pounced on a 1,100-man army of Loyalists. Despite the fact that the Loyalists were well dug in atop Kings Mountain on the border of the Carolinas, the over-mountain men defeated them. This was the first major British disaster in the south. They suf-

Nathanael Greene

fered 225 dead, 163 wounded and 716 taken prisoner. The over-mountain men suffered only 28 dead and 62 wounded. Suddenly, Loyalists stopped joining the British, and more citizens started enlisting on the side of the Revolution.

THE BATTLE OF COWPENS

Greene headed south with only a little over 1,600 soldiers, hardly the equal of Cornwallis' force. Greene hoped to gain numbers by drawing men from local militias. In January 1781, one of General Greene's commanders, General Daniel Morgan of Virginia, ran into a veteran group of British raiders under the leadership of a daring cavalry officer, Lieutenant Colonel

133

Henry "Light Horse Harry" Lee

Banastre Tarleton.

Morgan knew he was outmatched by Tarleton's 1,100 veteran British troops, who included about 200 cavalry. He retreated to a large, sloping cow pasture and cleverly deployed his troops in three lines. The first two lines were ordered to make a brief stand, then retreat. This would give the British the impression that they had the entire American army on the run.

In the first line, Morgan positioned 120 sharpshooters. Their job was to slow the enemy advance with some well-placed shots, then fall back. In the second line, Morgan placed his most inexperienced troops – 300 militiamen from Georgia and Carolina, untested in battle. He instructed them to take two shots each, then they were free to leave

the field of battle. In the third line, Morgan placed his crack Continental soldiers from Maryland and Delaware and his veteran Virginia militia, about 500 men in all. They would do most of the fighting.

The bewildered British hit the third line of veteran soldiers, and were stopped. Then the relatively new recruits from the second line – the Georgia and Carolina militia – returned to the field of battle and attacked again from the flanks.

The British line quickly collapsed. It was all over in an hour. The British losses were staggering – 110 dead, over 200 wounded, and 500 captured. The Americans lost only 12 men, with another 60 wounded.

This defeat was a major turning point in the war in the south. From this point on, it was easier for Greene to call for the support of local militia units in the Carolinas. Morgan's victory breathed new life into the patriot cause.

CORNWALLIS CHASES GREENE

Cornwallis had a difficult choice to make. He could either pull his forces back to the coast or take a chance that he could run down Greene and Morgan and defeat them in battle. Unable to accept defeat after only one American victory, Cornwallis set off after them. Greene employed Washington's tactics and took off northward through North Carolina.

The race was on, but the British

were notoriously slow. Cornwallis became frustrated that Greene and Morgan were outrunning his army. He ordered the destruction of some of his heavy equipment. As a result, the British did begin moving faster, but Greene's soldiers still managed to escape into Virginia. Cornwallis had chased his foe across the Carolinas and had nothing to show for it – except a worn-out army.

THE BATTLE OF GUILFORD COURTHOUSE

Once again, Greene adopted Washington's tactics. He suddenly turned back, and surprised Cornwallis at Guilford Courthouse, North Carolina. When the smoke had cleared, the Americans were forced to retreat, but the British had paid dearly. Twice as many British soldiers had fallen during the battle as Americans. The British had prevailed only because they had more men.

Now Cornwallis' army was exhausted and running low on supplies. Cornwallis was forced to turn towards the coast. He and his army ran for Wilmington, North Carolina, where the powerful British Navy could resupply him. With Cornwallis out of the way, Greene wasted no time regaining lost territory in the Carolinas.

And so by the end of 1780, the British were back where they had started in 1778, when they began their southern strategy by attacking Savannah, Georgia. They held only New York City and a few southern seaports.

MARCH 1781

Jed Warwick was crouched behind a split rail fence, shivering in the cold March dawn of 1781. He and his army companions had been fleeing from Lord Cornwallis for weeks. Jed was tired and hungry, but his nervous energy grew as the sun rose and melted the frost.

The British were coming. He could see their red ranks forming up for attack across the muddy cornfield before the fence. General Nathanael Greene had decided to finally make a stand, right there near tiny Guilford Courthouse in North Carolina. No more running.

General Cornwallis had written home, saying he "was tired of marching around the country in search of adventure." Now General Greene would give him more than an adventure.

"Try not to run until you have fired a couple of shots at 'em," Greene ordered his nervous militia. "After you've taken a couple of shots, fall back to the third line of Virginians behind you and do it again. After that, the third line of my Continentals will stop the British. Don't try to beat them all by yourselves."

It was a great relief to be commanded by a general who understood the fear the average soldier felt preparing to face those terrible British bayonets. Many had run from them at Camden, some all the way back home. To prevent that, General Greene had even stationed a few American sharpshooters behind the militia with orders to shoot the first man who ran before the order to retreat was given.

"I never used a bayonet before,"

whispered Jed's friend, John Crawford.

Jed did not even have a bayonet. "Me either," Jed answered, feeling a little lump beginning to rise in his throat.

The two heard a horseman gallop up behind them. It was Colonel Henry Lee – "Light Horse Harry" Lee of Virginia, they called him – prancing along on his pale gray horse.

"He looks about as feisty as a bantam rooster, don't he?" John chuckled under his breath.

Lee was just back from an attack before dawn on the British cavalry. Smiling, he shouted encouragement to the militia. "Don't worry, boys. I beat the lobsterbacks three times before breakfast, and we can sure do it again!"

Jed smiled nervously as some of the others cheered.

Suddenly the call rang out, "Load up!" Major Eaton shouted gruffly, "Here they come."

Burrump, burrump, bur, rump, rump, rump. Over and over again, the British drums tapped out the rolling march as even lines of Redcoats began to cross the field. As they stepped all together to the beat, their bayonet tips glittered in the sun.

Jed pulled the hammer of his musket back to half-cock and rested the long heavy barrel on a fence rail.

"Not yet. Not yet!" Major Eaton scolded. "Wait 'till they get closer."

Burrump, burrump, bur, rump, rump, rump. The red line grew larger, the beat of the drums faster.

"Aim!" Jed picked out a distant British officer near the front line. "FIRE!" The fence row protecting the Americans disappeared in a roar of white smoke as flames shot from hundreds of musket barrels.

Jed looked up. A few British soldiers toppled backward in the first row, but the volley had been fired from too far away. The officer he'd aimed at was still standing, waving his sword wildly and shouting to his men.

"Close up! Close up!" British Redcoats from the rear ranks came up smartly to fill the gaps.

"Load. Load," went the cry down the American line. Jed pulled his ramrod from below the barrel of his musket, reached back for a fresh cartridge in his knapsack, nervously tore the paper end off with his teeth and poured powder down the barrel, then inserted the round metal ball. With his ramrod, he rammed the ball all the way down the barrel, then dropped his ramrod. Seconds ticked by as slowly as minutes while Jed fumbled in the dirt to retrieve the ramrod.

When he looked up now he could make out the fierce expressions of the British as they had their own muskets lowered to their hips, bayonet tips seemingly pointed at only him.

Burrump, burrump, bur, rump, rump, rump. Men around Jed began to break for the line behind them. Jed took a few steps back, turned and quickly fired his musket over his shoulder, then ran to catch the rest. Fifty yards behind him, a British soldier moaned, grabbed his side and fell in front of the fence.

Jed and John puffed up to the second American line and took their places. They jammed home another shot

Using a firing arm in the 18th century required a great deal of training and very fast reflexes. A soldier would use his teeth to bite open a container of powder, place it carefully in the magazine, and then firmly ramrod the musket ball into the barrel. All the time, he was vulnerable to the attack of the enemy.

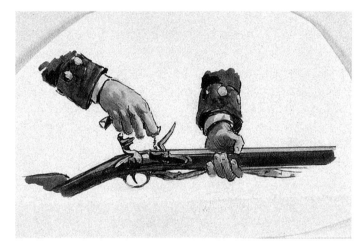

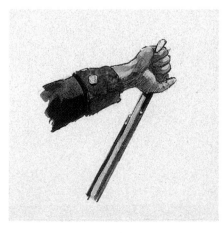

with their ramrods. Their officers stood just behind them, pacing back and forth, staring hard at anyone who was not standing firm. Jed filled his firing pan with powder, cocked the hammer of his musket, and watched the British coming over the fence that a minute earlier had been their front line.

"Aim!" Jed shouldered his musket and looked down the barrel at no one in particular – just a red blur closing on him. "FIRE!" Again the American line disappeared in musket smoke, causing groans from across the field as many more Redcoats fell to the ground.

The same British officer Jed had missed was screaming new orders. Dropping to one knee, the British soldiers raised their muskets. "FIRE" was the last thing Jed heard before explosive noise covered him. The whine of a ball passed by his left ear. The sickening THUD of shot hitting flesh around him made him wince as many of his own friends now fell to the ground, groaning in agony.

"Jed ... I'm hit!" John screamed as he clutched his leg. Jed saw a ragged tear in the cloth of his pants quickly fill with blood. "Run ... Jed ... Run!" Many were already running to the rear, heading for the last line of Greene's hardened Continentals at the top of the hill. There they stood grimly with fixed bayonets.

But some of Jed's militia weren't stopping there. They threw down their muskets and ran for the woods. They had had enough terror for one day. Jed looked down at John. Ignoring his screams, he picked him up.

"Hold on. You can make it," Jed

yelled as he put his arm around his limping friend and hustled him towards the safety of the third line.

Suddenly, Jed felt John slump. His friend was hit again. "Leave me. Save yourself, Jed. I'm a goner," John blurted out.

Feeling the strength of rage pour through his body, Jed picked John completely off the ground, threw him over his shoulder like a very heavy bag of flour and stumbled toward the rear for help. Cannon balls began throwing up earth all around them. The British had brought up their heavy guns.

Jed laid John down gently behind the slope of a hill well behind the front lines, then gave him his canteen of water. Jed still clutched his musket but felt at his side for his powder horn. It was lost in all the confusion. He took John's powder horn and turned back toward the crest of the hill, his young eyes narrowed in anger like slits of fire, glowing from his face blackened with powder stains. His hand no longer shook as he reloaded his musket.

Jed took his place among some other Virginians who were picking off the Hessian soldiers who were now closest to their part of the line. They were colorful targets, dressed in blue, fighting alongside the British regulars. Jed could hear the Hessians cursing in German as some of the Americans from the first line who had retreated to the side now pelted them with a deadly crossfire.

A rifleman took careful aim at Cornwallis and squeezed the trigger. Across the field, the British commander's horse fell dead beneath him. Cornwallis jumped up in a rage, grabbed another horse and pressed forward. Loose saddlebags on his new mount kept getting caught in the wild undergrowth of bushes. Finally a British sergeant grabbed the reins of Cornwallis' mount and forced the general back to safety.

Jed gave the British credit, despite their losses, for being well disciplined. They just kept coming. From his vantage point, positioned with the riflemen, Jed could no longer make out the lines of friend from enemy as the two sides struggled in hand-to-hand combat. Jed and the riflemen continued firing whenever they could pick out an enemy soldier or officer from the ongoing battle. He saw the British officer he'd fired at earlier make a lunge with his sword, miss, then fall to the ground, a victim of their fire.

The battle seemed to go on and on, but it was clear that the British Army was getting the worst of it. Suddenly, in disbelief, Jed watched while British cannon were turned about, pointed towards the front lines – pointed towards the backs of their own soldiers.

"He's going to fire into his own men,"

said the boy next to him. Jed gasped. With a roll of thunder, the cannon sprayed out hot grapeshot through the swarming mass of soldiers, killing friend and foe alike. The Americans were stunned. They began to disengage and pull back to the safety of the woods.

Jed moved back up the hill to find out about John. He ran into his commander, Colonel Campbell. "Is John dead?" Jed asked hesitantly.

"No, son, he was lucky. But his leg had to be cut off to stop the bleeding."

Jed winced at the thought. Battlefield leg amputations inflicted terrible pain.

"Come on, soldier," yelled an officer. "We've got to get back across the river."

It began to rain and Jed felt like crying. General Greene rode past, offering encouragement. He looked so tired. "Men, you did all that was asked, and more. But I could not risk your defeat. You are all the army we've got. But remember, we fight, get beat, then rise and fight again. The British can't take this forever."

On the British side, an exhausted General Cornwallis wrote a friend, "I never saw such fighting since God made me."

At the official surrender at Yorktown, Virginia, Cornwallis prepares to present his sword to George Washington. The artist actually created a scene that did not exist. In reality, Cornwallis sent a substitute to complete the surrender, and in turn, Washington asked one of his officers to accept the sword. At left, the first painting of George Washington seen by the people of France. It was painted by Jean-Baptiste Le Paon circa 1779.

Chapter 15

Yorktown: The Final American Victory

CORNWALLIS HEADS FOR VIRGINIA

Britain's southern strategy had been dealt a serious setback. The ground swell of support for the British had been blunted by American victories at Kings Mountain and Cowpens. Now Cornwallis made a fatal decision. He decided to head up into Virginia. In

New York, General Clinton was angry. He had ordered Cornwallis specifically to hold the Carolinas.

Throughout the summer of 1781, Cornwallis skirmished with militia units in Virginia and tried to find additional support from the local population. But Virginians were unimpressed. Cornwallis also attempted to convince General Clinton that his move into

Virginia was sound and worthy of support. Eventually Clinton did send reinforcements to Cornwallis, raising his army to 7,000 men.

THE BATTLE OF YORKTOWN

At the end of the summer, Cornwallis located his new army in Yorktown, just outside Williamsburg. There, it could be easily resupplied by the British fleet from New York.

Far to the north, a large French army had landed in New England to join General Washington. Commanded by General Comte de Rochambeau, the French forces were eager to help the Americans. Washington and Rochambeau were looking for ways to attack the British in New York City when an opportunity came to strike in Virginia.

A messenger from Admiral de Grasse, commander of the French fleet operating in the West Indies, arrived at Washington's headquarters near New York City. The admiral said that the French fleet could be spared for a few months to help Washington and Rochambeau, and asked where they wanted him to bring it. The two generals quickly formulated a plan. If de Grasse could place his fleet at the mouth of the Chesapeake Bay, he would cut off Cornwallis from the British supply ships in New York. Then the French and American armies could attack at Yorktown without fear of meeting British reinforcements. Rochambeau placed all of his soldiers under Washington's command, making

the total fighting force very powerful.

In September 1781, Washington hurriedly put his strengthened army on the road, by heading south to Virginia. He again deceived the British by making his troop movements appear as though the Americans and French were about to attack New York City itself. Clinton was fooled. He braced himself for the attack.

But Washington quickly marched his entire army right by New York City, to the top of the Chesapeake Bay. There, some of his troops boarded ships and sailed south to reinforce the small American army outside Yorktown. The rest of the men marched there over land. By September 28, 1781, Washington had over 16,000 soldiers at Yorktown, half of whom were French troops. They successfully settled into positions and laid siege to the British defenses. Cornwallis was trapped with his back to the sea.

Washington was not the type of commander who stayed safely in the rear of the fighting. His lack of fear during battle was once again displayed at Yorktown. During one day of heavy British cannon fire, a soldier named John Suddarth looked up from digging a trench to see that Washington had taken a death-defying position. He had taken his telescope:

> ...and mounted the highest, most prominent and most exposed part of our fortifications and there stood exposed to the enemy's fire, where shot seemed flying almost as thick as hail

and were instantly demolishing portions of the embankment around him.

Washington survived without injury, however. Soon the British, seeing they were outnumbered, abandoned their outer defenses and withdrew to their primary fortifications. From New York, Clinton sent word to Cornwallis that he was sending 5,000 reinforcements from his 15,000-man army stationed in New York City. Unfortunately for the British, the reinforcements never arrived. The British ran into the French fleet, headed by Admiral de Grasse, which had positioned itself to block off access to the Chesapeake Bay and Yorktown. After a large naval battle off the Virginia Capes, British naval commanders realized they lacked the force to fight their way to rescue Cornwallis.

Over the coming weeks, Washington's army tightened its hold on Yorktown while General Henry Knox's artillery rained a constant stream of death down on the British. As one American described the scene:

...when a shell falls...I have more than once witnessed fragments of

The surrender at Yorktown, October 19, 1781. Washington sits on a brown horse to the right. His deputy, Major General Benjamin Lincoln, on the white horse, actually received the surrender.

mangled bodies and limbs of the British soldiers thrown into the air by the bursting of our shells.

From inside the British defenses by the York River, a shell-shocked soldier described how:

we could not find refuge in or out of the town. The people fled to the waterside and hid in hastily contrived shelters on the banks, but many were killed by bursting bombs.

Finally, with supplies running out and some of the fortifications already in American hands, Cornwallis decided he must abandon Yorktown. He attempted to retreat across the York River, but a sudden storm drove back many of the small boats Cornwallis had seized to ferry his army across, and damaged the rest. Wishing to avoid further blood-shed, Cornwallis decided to surrender. He sadly wrote General Clinton in New York:

I cannot recommend that the fleet and army should run great risk in endeavoring to save us.

On October 19, 1781, the British army surrendered to the Americans. The British marched down between row upon row of French and American soldiers drawn into formation to receive the surrender. Britain had lost another army.

In Britain, King George III wanted to fight on. But the British Prime Minister, Lord North, realized Yorktown was the end. He took the bad news, as one person described it, "like a ball in the breast."

"Oh God! It is all over!" North moaned again and again.

Parliament told the King to end the war. Wars are expensive and taxes had never been higher. British merchants were also pressuring Parliament to end the war so they could resume trade. In the end, once the peace treaty was signed in Paris in 1783, the United States of America had won its independence, as well as all the land east of the Mississippi except for Florida and a narrow strip of land along the southern coast.

OCTOBER 21, 1781

The Warwick family had gathered in church in Stanley Hundred. Services were almost over, and the preacher was giving his benediction.

Almighty God, we thank you for bestowing victory at Yorktown. May your hand guide General Washington and all the soldiers of his army. Continue to watch over our brave men. In Thy name we pray this. Amen.

Jed was still in his uniform, sword at his side. The uniform was a bit ragged and had patches where it had been mended in camp. Its colors were no longer bright but drab in places. The mud stains had been pretty much brushed out, but they still showed as brownish areas.

In spite of his appearance, Patience

A ceremonial sword owned by General George Washington.

and Michael were proud of their father as they stood in the churchyard on that sunny Sunday morning in October. All the congregation came by to congratulate him on the Army's great victory at Yorktown. Their friends, the Bakers, had driven from Williamsburg to go to church with the Warwicks on that special day.

"It was a wonderful victory," proclaimed William Baker.

"It's not over yet," cautioned Jed. "But I don't think the King's heart will be in it for much longer – to say nothing of the British soldiers' hearts," Jed laughed, and so did everyone else.

Jed explained the surrender scene to everyone within earshot. "It was a grand spectacle to see the British Army drawn up in parade formation, flags no longer flying. We were lined up with the French soldiers opposite us. The Redcoats' band began playing a song called 'The World Turned Upside Down,' someone told me it was. Anyway, the words fit the occasion perfectly." Then Jed recited the lines to his friend.

If ponies rode men and if grass ate cows,
And cats should be chased into holes by the mouse ...
If summer were spring and the other way around,
Then all the world would be upside down.

145

"And I'll wager that's how King George will feel when he hears about it!" William Baker laughed, and the crowd joined in.

"And the Redcoats took their loss in ill humor," said Jed. "When they got to the field where they had to surrender their weapons, they just threw 'em into a pile so hard that many muskets broke in pieces. Some of them were crying and most wouldn't even look us in the eye – that is until young General Lafayette ordered the band to play "Yankee Doodle." That snapped their heads around! Oh how the British used to laugh at us about how silly we looked. They'd sing that song:

Yankee Doodle rode to town a' sitting on a pony. Stuck a feather in his cap and called it macaroni.

Jed turned to his neighbors to address them in a loud voice so all could hear. "Thank you all for your support and your prayers during this struggle. Now, if you'll excuse us, I have to be back to my regiment tonight, and we have some chickens at home that are in need of frying before then. Good-bye to you all."

PROBLEMS OVER ARMY PAY

After the surrender of Cornwallis at

General Washington says an emotional goodbye to his officers in December 1783.

Yorktown on October 19, 1781, George Washington and his army returned northward to keep watch on Clinton's army, still sitting in New York City. The French soldiers followed later. Over the next year, the Continental Army just sat and waited for the peace treaty to be negotiated. Gradually, morale declined. Now, with no enemy to fight, both soldiers and officers began to complain about their lack of pay.

The Continental Congress had consistently failed to keep the soldiers properly supplied or paid. Most merely wanted to be paid what was owed them, then released from service to return home. The officers, on the other hand, wanted Congress to give them a pension that amounted to half-pay for life. This was not an unreasonable demand. Congress had promised them the money two years earlier, but now gave no indication that it intended to make good on that commitment.

The officers made a compromise proposal that amounted to a lump cash payment delivered when they left the Army. But the government had no money, so Congress remained silent. Some politicians suggested that the agreements made by Congress should be paid by the individual states, not by Congress, but the states would not pay the soldiers either.

CIVILIAN OR MILITARY RULE

Talk began to spread that the Army itself should march on Congress over the pay issue. The threatened mutiny was generally called the Newburgh Conspiracy. When Washington heard of the threat, he denounced it. Never would an army that he commanded be used against the civil government.

To his officers, in a meeting at Newburgh, New York on March 15, 1783, he pledged he would work to ensure that Congress treated them justly and cautioned them not to do anything that would "lessen the dignity, and sully the glory you have hereto maintained." The appeal was well-reasoned and swayed some, but then came the moment that most touched the soldiers and officers assembled. Washington faltered while reading his notes. Reaching for his glasses, he looked up and remarked:

> Gentlemen, you will permit me to put on my spectacles, for I have not only grown gray, but almost blind in the service of my country.

However much the Army had suffered, he had suffered right along with them. Old veterans remembered Washington standing in the sleet along the Delaware River that Christmas in 1776 as his troops prepared to strike Trenton. Others recalled that Washington had lived in a simple tent at Valley Forge until all his soldiers had cabins for shelter. At Yorktown, he had dug the first spade of soil to open the siege. He had written to Congress demanding that his soldiers be paid fairly for their faithful service. If not, "then shall I have learned what ingratitude is: then shall I have realized a tale which will embitter every moment of my future life."

As a result of Washington's resolve, the Newburgh Conspiracy ended abruptly. Washington had set a principle maintained by the United States military down to the present day — namely that the military would remain ever the servant of the people and of its civilian government, and never its oppressor.

KING WASHINGTON?

One of Washington's officers posed another solution to the problems of unifying the new nation. In May of 1782, he wrote General Washington suggesting that the Army march on Congress and install Washington as the new king of America.

Washington was shocked. He wrote back that he viewed the idea "with abhorrence," and ordered the officer to "banish these thoughts from your mind."

The peace negotiations dragged on for months — even years. Finally, in November 1783, word came to Washington that a treaty had finally been signed a few weeks earlier in Paris. The last British soldiers left New York City on November 25, and Washington marched in to replace them later that same day.

About a week later, Washington said good-bye to his officers and started the journey home to Mount Vernon. He was now 51 years old. He had first entered military service 30 years earlier. Since then, he had lived most of his life in the public eye.

On the way home from New York, Washington stopped by Annapolis, Maryland, where the Congress was then meeting, on December 23, 1783. The group had been frightened out of Philadelphia by soldiers threatening to take action over back pay due them. Washington's resignation as commander in chief of the army was delivered in the old Annapolis Statehouse.

Washington wrote ahead to Congress, telling them of his plans to resign and asking them "whether it be in writing, or at an audience." Following the instructions Congress returned to him, he presented himself at noon before the elegant brick statehouse which overlooked the harbor. Washington took a seat below the 18 congressmen. By arrangement, they did not stand when he entered, nor did they even remove their hats. Washington was to bow to them upon entering and leaving. It was all to demonstrate the supremacy of the elected officials — Congress — over the military authority — Washington.

The white-pillared gallery above the chamber was filled with women while prominent gentlemen lined yellow walls below. The rustle of the spectators was hushed by the Secretary's command, "Silence!" One of Washington's former aides, James McHenry, described how the group was transfixed by Washington's parting words:

The past, the present, the manner, the occasion, all conspired to render it a

Perhaps the greatest moment of Washington's career was his resignation as commander in chief. He remains one of the only victorious military leaders in history to voluntarily surrender all his power, just when his soldiers were hoping to make him king.

spectacle inexpressibly solemn and affecting.

The President of Congress gave Washington his arranged cue: "Sir, the United States in Congress assembled are prepared to receive your communications." The Virginian rose and bowed respectfully. As he began to read his remarks, his hand shook. The tremor of the paper increased as he thanked his "family" of officers, his words building toward the unbearable:

> I consider it an indispensable duty to close this last solemn act of my official life by commending the interests of our dearest country to Almighty God, and those who have the superintendence of them to His holy blessing...

Washington faltered, his voice sank, and in silence the packed room felt his anguish. He grabbed his paper with both hands to steady it. According to McHenry: "The spectators all wept and there was hardly a member of Congress who did not drop tears." Collecting himself, Washington resumed in the most penetrating manner,

> Having now finished the work assigned me, I retire from the great theatre of action, and, bidding an affectionate farewell to this august body under whose orders I have so long acted, I here offer my commission and take my leave of all of the employments of public life.

Washington's remarks had taken a little over three minutes. He handed the Secretary a copy of his remarks and bowed to the President of Congress and the other members. The legislators remained seated, but they all tipped their hats as Washington walked out of the chamber, down the hall, and out onto the pillared porch toward Frances Street where his horse was waiting. Washington wanted to depart immediately in order to make it home to Mount Vernon – some 50 miles away – by the next day, Christmas Eve.

Benjamin West, an American artist working in London, told of a conversation he had with King George III. The King asked him what George Washington would do if America won the war. West said he supposed Washington would return to his farm. "If he does that," the King remarked, "he will be the greatest man in the world."

The symbolism of Washington's act was very important in American history. It laid the foundation for civilian rule – that is, rule by elected officials, instead of by a military ruler or king. Washington had rejected many offers to become the new king of America. Now, all he wanted to do was to go into retirement and live a quiet life at home. He arrived in time to spend Christmas with his family.

Over the coming months, the Continental Army gradually disbanded. Its soldiers found their way home as best they could. Joseph Plum Martin, a Continental soldier from Connecticut, wrote of the sorrow he felt in parting from his fellow soldiers:

I confess, after all, that my anticipation of the happiness I should experience upon such a day as this was not realized.... We had lived together as a family of brothers for several years, setting aside some little family squabbles like most other families, had shared with each other the hardships, dangers and sufferings incidental to a soldier's life; had sympathized with each other in trouble and sickness; had assisted in bearing each other's burdens or strove to make them lighter by council and advice; had endeavored to conceal each other's faults or make them appear in as good a light as they would bear.... And now we were to be, the greater part of us, parted forever; as unconditionally separated as though the grave lay between us.... Ah! it was a serious time.

Unfortunately, most of the American soldiers had no money for the trip home. Returning penniless, they depended on handouts to help them on their journey.

But they had won a great victory. It was through their sacrifices that independence had been achieved and a new nation would soon be created – the United States of America.

150

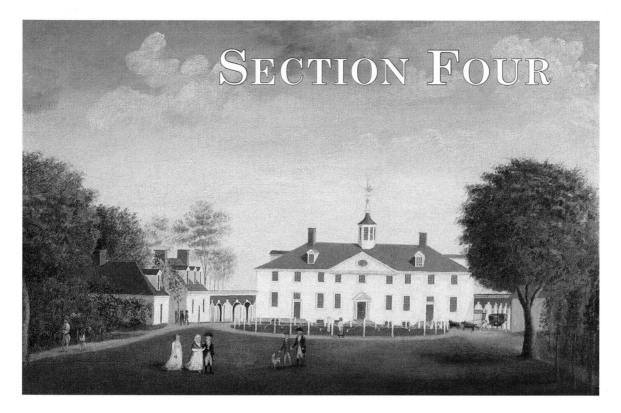

SECTION FOUR

THE ARTICLES OF CONFEDERATION
AND THE CONSTITUTION

George Washington's home, Mount Vernon, is where he hoped to retire following the long years of the Revolutionary War. But he could not deny the call of his country and agreed to serve two terms as president.

Carpenter's Hall in Philadelphia was one of several sites where the Founding Fathers formulated some of the most important documents our world has ever known. At left is the Pennsylvania State House, known today as Independence Hall.

Chapter 16

The Articles of Confederation

After the outbreak of fighting in Boston in 1775, the British colonial governments began to crumble. One by one, the royal governors and their advisors reluctantly returned to England. The Second Continental Congress passed a resolution urging the colonies to organize new governments to replace British leaders. John Adams, the Massachusetts delegate who would serve as President 22 years later, called this "the most important resolution that was ever taken in America."

Gradually, the patriots in the individual colonies began to pick up the pieces and reorganize their governments by writing their own state constitutions. The democratic ideas expressed by Jefferson in the Declaration of Independence found their way into the new state constitutions as well. Many new state constitutions began with a bill of rights. These documents declared that the people had the right to religious freedom, free speech, free press, freedom to assemble to protest against government actions, the right to a fair trial, and the right of equal treatment. Not all people were considered when these rights were declared. Slaves, Native Americans, women and those who owned no property did not enjoy these freedoms under the law.

Americans, though, had essentially decreed that they would not be governed by the opinion or whim of a king. America would be ruled by laws — written laws which every person could see and understand. Over a century earlier, Britain had moved towards a similar rule of law with its own revolution. The British revolution had established that Parliament was the law-making body, not the King. But in America there would be no king at all. America was the first nation to experiment with an entirely new form of government — a government of laws, consented to by its citizens. In America, the whims of a few would not dictate to the majority.

THE SEPARATION OF POWERS CONCEPT

In order to prevent one person from gaining too much power, the new state leaders began to develop an idea known as the separation of powers concept. The powers of government would be spread out among several groups. Many people share power in the American system. The different branches of government serve as checks and balances to prevent any one branch from getting too much power.

Where did this idea come from? Many of the leaders in the states were influenced by people like the great French political writer, Montesquieu. He believed that "men entrusted with power tend to abuse it." He also stated that the best form of government divided its power among a number of agencies.

As a result, after the Revolution, state governments established three basic branches: the executive, the legislative, and the judicial. The executive branch is headed by the governor of the state. His job is to oversee the government generally. Now here's where the checks and balances system comes into play. Although the chief executive of a state – the governor – suggests legislation, only the legislature can pass it. The legislature can make the laws, but if the governor feels a law is bad, he can veto, or block it. If the legislators think the governor is wrong to veto a law, they can pass it anyway over his objections if a large percentage of their members agree to do so.

Here's another example: in many states just after the Revolution, even the legislature itself was divided into two houses, an upper house and a lower house. The purpose of this was to further divide the power of the legislative branch.

Meanwhile, the judicial branch of government keeps a watchful eye on new legislation, making certain that the new laws do not trample on anyone's basic rights as set forth in the bill of rights of the state constitution.

One reason the American system of

government is so stable is that the separation of powers concept was built into the original constitutions of all the states in the United States. This also became the basic concept in the federal constitution as well. Under governments which have chosen the rule of law, rather than the rule of a king, these two concepts – separation of powers and checks and balances – are the foundation of freedom. Without a balance of power nothing can eventually take place but a dictatorship, or a return to the rule of a king.

SEPARATION OF CHURCH AND STATE

One of the most cherished aspects of the American experiment has been the separation of church and state. This concept does not mean that religion should be eliminated from the American way of life. During the Revolution, it meant that people should not be forced to pay taxes to a state church or be told by government how they should worship. In other words, it meant government should stay out of our religious life.

For example, before the Revolutionary War broke out, the people in nine of the thirteen colonies were required to pay taxes for the support of an official state church. This idea originated in Europe. There, the government designated an official state religion, and the citizens had to support that church, even if they belonged to a different one. In Spain, France, and Portugal, the state religion was the Roman Catholic Church. In England, the official church was the Protestant Anglican Church. In European history, people were frequently killed or tortured for believing in a religion which was different from the one approved by the government.

RELIGIOUS TOLERANCE

Gradually, America became the testing ground for another new concept – religious tolerance. A man named Roger Williams championed the idea long before the American Revolution. In 1633, Williams argued from his pulpit in Salem, Massachusetts, that everyone had the God-given right to worship as they pleased. He understood that you could not force someone to believe or worship in a certain way.

Hearing this, church officials planned to send him back to England, but Williams escaped from Massachusetts colony and went a bit further south, where he founded Providence, Rhode Island. Rhode Island is small in size, but large in significance. It became a symbol for religious tolerance in America and the entire world. The Rhode Island Charter of 1663 became the model for the rest of the colonies. It read in part:

No person within the ... colony, at any time hereafter, shall be ... molested, punished ... or called in question for any differences in opinion in matters of religion.

After the American Revolution, the

principle of religious toleration grew stronger and the state-sponsored churches grew weaker. By 1787, official churches existed in only three states: New Hampshire, Massachusetts, and Connecticut. Eventually, they disappeared in those states as well. Since then, freedom from government interference in the way we worship has been one of the cornerstones of American democracy.

SLAVERY

The first black slaves were brought to the British colony of Virginia as early as 1619. That means that by the time of the Revolution, slavery had existed in America for over 150 years. Slavery was mostly confined to the southern states where large farm operations needed lots of inexpensive labor to raise crops. However, slavery did exist in northern states as well. New York, for example, did not abolish slavery until the 1820s.

Many northerners came to oppose slavery. They thought it was wrong that America would be fighting for freedom on one hand while allowing slavery on the other. But southerners viewed slavery as crucial to the economic success of their region. The big plantation owners felt they couldn't succeed without slavery. However, there were many exceptions. Patrick Henry of Virginia spoke out against slavery, saying it was "inconsistent with the Bible and destructive of liberty." In fact, some southern slave owners freed their slaves voluntarily. George Washington did so upon his death.

George and Martha Washington owned more than 300 slaves who worked on five adjoining farms. Near the end of his life, Washington began to write to his colleagues that slaves should not exist in a truly free society. He freed his slaves in his will. There now exists a memorial at Mount Vernon that recognizes the contributions of slaves to our nation, and an event is organized each year to honor the slaves by Black Women United for Action.

Not all black people were slaves. Some had escaped from their masters or purchased their own freedom. Some free blacks were the children or grandchildren of free men and women. Many free blacks, in fact, fought in the Continental Army. By 1778, the names of 780 of them were counted in 14 different army regiments. Many more served on the high seas on naval privateers. It is estimated that, altogether, about 5,000 served.

Although the Continental Congress banned the slave trade for a period of time after the war, it eventually gave in to southern pressure to allow it. After the Revolution was over, some states adopted laws which gradually freed the slaves. But in spite of attempts to abolish it, slavery continued throughout most of America after the Revolution.

Even though democratic principles were expressed in the Declaration of Independence, America was still not as free as it is today. Remember, this was a great political experiment. Americans had taken a long step towards democracy, but there was much that remained to be done.

Indeed, the American Revolution is still going on. You see, the Revolution wasn't just the military battles of George Washington's times. The Revolution created a new concept — government of the people, by the people, and for the people. Today, Americans continue to lead the world in defining rights for our citizens and responsibilities for our government.

That's what one of the signers of the

Dr. Benjamin Rush in a portrait by Charles Willson Peale.

Declaration of Independence, Dr. Benjamin Rush, meant when he said: "The American war is over, but this is far from being the case with the American Revolution."

DR. BENJAMIN RUSH (1745-1813)

Dr. Benjamin Rush was the most influential physician in America. He graduated from Princeton University at age 15 and received his degree in medicine at age 23 from the University of Edinburgh, Scotland.

Back in America, he set up the first free clinic in the United States. He also helped found the first anti-slavery society.

During the Revolutionary War, Dr. Rush served as the top doctor (the Surgeon General) in the Continental

Army. Later, he served as treasurer of the U.S. Mint.

THE NEED FOR UNITY

By the start of 1784, the former 13 British colonies were suddenly independent of Great Britain. Now they had to learn how to govern themselves by cooperating with each other. During the Revolution and for the next few years America went through a very confusing, difficult time trying to decide what kind of national government should be established.

During the war, the delegates to the Second Continental Congress had long debates over the issues that faced them. For example, Congress could not tax. It could only request funds from the states. When action was needed, all Congress could do was to pass a resolution urging each of the states to act in a certain manner. If any of the state legislatures decided not to accept its recommendation, the Continental Congress had no power to make them comply. In other words, the national government was very, very weak during this period after the Revolution. To most Americans, that was just the way they wanted it. They had experienced a strong central government in the form of Great Britain, and they wanted no more of that.

ARTICLES OF CONFEDERATION

With a war to fight, Congress agreed that some kind of unity was necessary. A week after the Declaration of Independence was signed, a committee headed by John Dickinson of Pennsylvania presented a plan called "Articles of Confederation and Perpetual Union." Not until 16 months later, however, in November 1777, did the delegates vote to adopt the plan. Many factors made the Articles very unpopular. In fact, it took another four years, until 1781, to convince all the states to accept the Articles.

The Articles of Confederation created a confederation, or loose-knit association of the states, called, for the first time, the United States of America.

THE LAND QUESTION

Many problems delayed acceptance of the Articles of Confederation, but the biggest stumbling block was the question of who would own the land between the Appalachian Mountains and the Mississippi River. During the war, this land was under British control and was claimed by several states.

Small states like New Jersey, Delaware, and Maryland had no claims to this land. They complained that without western lands, they would not be able to expand, and the larger states would dominate the new union. Maryland insisted that it would not join the Confederation unless all the states gave up claims to this land. This problem could easily have prevented the cooperation necessary to mold an effective union.

Virginia claimed the largest block of western land. The Governor of Virginia, Thomas Jefferson, offered a compromise. He agreed to give up Virginia's claims to some of the land west of the mountains. This meant that other states could give up their claims without fearing that Virginia would be much larger than they were. After that, all of the states finally agreed to the plan of union.

PROBLEMS WITH THE ARTICLES OF CONFEDERATION

The problems of the new government became apparent almost at once. The state delegations in the Confederation Congress could rarely agree on anything, and so they passed few laws. As a result, most of the states saw the central government as ineffective. The states acted autonomously, that is, they acted like independent countries.

This was a big problem when it came to money and trade. Each state printed its own money. One state's money was not accepted in some other states. Some states' money was worth more than others. For example, a Virginia £ note was worth more than a Pennsylvania or a Maryland £ note. Some states passed high taxes on products imported from other states in order to protect local manufacturers. This created economic chaos, especially for those whose business relied heavily on interstate trade.

Another big problem was the power to tax. Taxation was one of the root causes of the break from Great Britain. The states were not anxious to give any

central government the power to tax. Consequently, raising the funds to carry on the normal operations of a government was very difficult. Some states refused to pay the central government any tax money. If a state refused to pay, Congress could do nothing about it.

Lack of authority to tax had serious consequences. There was not enough money for the important work that needed to be done. For instance, the national government had to deliver the mail between states, and send ambassadors out to other countries. And it had to take care of the continuing warfare with the Indians in the western lands. There were also problems with Britain and Spain.

PROBLEMS WITH BRITAIN AND SPAIN

The British refused to withdraw from the forts and trading posts they had established in the area which would later become the states of Ohio, Indiana, Michigan, Illinois, Wisconsin, and parts of Minnesota. Even worse, some reckless British officers supplied the Indians with guns and ammunition and encouraged them to attack the American settlers. Congress was powerless to stop this.

The Spanish, who owned all the land west of the Mississippi River, refused to allow Americans access to the port of New Orleans, where the Mississippi River flowed into the Gulf of Mexico. This port was very important to the settlers of the Ohio River valley,

General Benjamin Lincoln

THE ANNAPOLIS CONVENTION

By 1785, many people were worried about the future of the new nation. They wondered if the states would eventually break away to form into separate countries or even rejoin Great Britain.

George Washington saw that the new nation was in trouble. A meeting between delegates from Virginia and Maryland was held in his home at Mount Vernon. So many national concerns arose at this meeting that the delegates agreed to recommend to the other states that they all meet the next year in Annapolis, Maryland, to discuss solutions.

One of the principal advocates of a stronger national government was James Madison, a young Virginian. He played a leading role in getting the Virginia assembly to issue the call for the state delegations to meet in Annapolis. Madison received encouragement from Washington and other prominent Virginians.

Attendance at the Annapolis Convention in September 1786 was disappointing. Only five states sent delegates. Those who attended were strong nationalists – that is, they favored the creation of a stronger central government. From this convention came a recommendation to try again. The delegates called for a meeting in Philadelphia the following spring.

This proposal might not have gathered much support had it not been for the threat of civil war in Massachusetts in the fall of 1786.

for example. There were few good roads from the east coast of the American colonies across the Appalachian Mountains. Settlers in the west had no way to sell their products except to float them down the Mississippi on crude rafts and sell them to the Spanish in New Orleans. Again, the American Congress was too weak to do anything.

SHAYS' REBELLION - 1786

Following the Revolution, America experienced an economic slump. The farmers of Massachusetts were especially hard hit. Many of them were deeply in debt. Much of their cash income had come from the sale of their farm produce to the British West Indies. After the war, this market was closed to them, and so they found it increasingly difficult to pay their taxes and debts.

To make matters worse, businessmen, mostly from Boston, controlled the state legislature. They managed to pass new laws which increased the share of taxes the farmers had to pay. Soon the farmers began to have their lands seized for nonpayment of taxes and sold at auction by the government.

Many of the farmers were former soldiers and officers in Washington's army. They became angry and threatened to stop the taking of their lands unless the Massachusetts legislature did something to give them some relief. But the legislature refused to act.

A group of farmers banded together. They surrounded courthouses and demanded that the judges stop foreclosing mortgages and seizing farm property. Their leader was a veteran of the Battle of Bunker's Hill, Captain Daniel Shays. The countryside of Massachusetts was on the verge of civil war. A group of men led by Shays attacked the federal arsenal at Springfield. This was a place where guns, cannon, and powder had been stored after the Revolution. But the men were too poorly armed to succeed. This was known as Shay's Rebellion.

Soon, the merchants in Boston raised funds to equip an army led by General Benjamin Lincoln, one of Washington's veteran commanders. Lincoln's army soon crushed Shays' Rebellion and chased many of the men westward into what is now Vermont. But still, the new nation was on the verge of chaos, and Washington knew it. "There are combustibles in every state which a spark might set fire to," he wrote.

Shays' Rebellion made people in every state realize that the Articles of Confederation were not working and something had to be done – and soon! Now, the Philadelphia Convention in the spring of 1787 took on new importance. When it convened in May, delegates from 12 states were there or on the way. Only Rhode Island declined to participate.

Washington, standing on the raised platform, presides at the Constitutional Convention. As presiding officer, Washington seldom lent his voice to the debates that raged through the hot summer months, but his presence kept the Convention together. At times during the proceedings it looked as though the 55 delegates would never reach any sort of compromise. At left, a superb portrait of Washington by Charles Willson Peale.

Chapter 17

The Constitutional Convention

Not everyone thought the Philadelphia Convention, called to review and revise the Articles of Confederation, was a good idea. Many Americans were suspicious of what the Convention might do. Rhode Island would not participate at all. Patrick Henry was elected as one of Virginia's delegates, but refused to attend, reportedly saying that he "smelt a rat."

Despite the initial criticism, on May 14, 1787, the doors of Philadelphia's State House (later known as Independence Hall) were opened to the delegates of what would later be called the Constitutional Convention. However, only two delegations appeared on opening day – one from Virginia, led by George Washington, and one from Pennsylvania, led by Benjamin Franklin. By May 25, however, delegates from seven states – a majority – had appeared and the most famous convention in American history got under way.

The 55 delegates who attended the Constitutional Convention included many remarkable younger men. Benjamin Franklin was the "elder statesman" at age 81. George

Washington was one of the older members at age 55. James Madison of Virginia was only 36. Alexander Hamilton just 30. Most of them had taken some role in the American Revolution. More than half had been members of Congress. Eight had signed the Declaration of Independence eleven years earlier.

SECRECY

The Convention unanimously elected George Washington to be its president, or presiding officer. He would organize and run the daily debate. The delegates also agreed that the meetings of the Convention would be held in secret. Guards were posted at every door. Each member agreed not to discuss the business of the Convention with outsiders.

Why the secrecy? Because the delegates knew that news of the issues being debated would quickly spread. They also knew that it would be easier to iron out differences of opinion in private than in a public debate. They wanted all members to feel free to express their ideas honestly, without fear that their opinions would be reported to the press even before the members themselves could reach decisions. So, secrecy was really the only way to ensure an honest look at the issues for the good of the entire nation.

Secrecy was so tight that some of the delegates were worried about the aging and talkative Benjamin Franklin. They knew he loved dinner parties and they were afraid he might absent-mindedly divulge the confidential deliberations. So wherever he went he was accompanied by another member of the delegation to restrain him if he accidentally began to talk about the Convention's affairs.

AREAS OF AGREEMENT

At the start of the Constitutional Convention, the delegates generally agreed on three things:

1. That a mere revision of the Articles of Confederation would not solve the nation's problems. An entirely new Constitution was needed.
2. That a stronger central government was needed. They recognized that no federal government would be respected by the states unless it had the powers to tax, regulate commerce, and raise an army.
3. That safeguards had to be put in place to prevent the new central government from becoming dictatorial. The members had to be sure that no single group of people could gain and hold power, and thereby dominate the rest against their will.

AREAS OF DISAGREEMENT

The major problem the delegates to the Constitutional Convention faced was how power would be shared between the larger states and the smaller states. The larger states felt that since they had a greater population they should have a larger percentage of the votes in Congress. The smaller states argued that they had no reason to join a union in which their voice would be insignificant compared to the larger states. A second major area of disagreement was over issues related to the keeping of slaves. Yet another was about the size and control of the army.

THE VIRGINIA PLAN

When the states agreed to send delegates to Philadelphia, they did so for "the sole and express purpose of revising the Articles of Confederation." However, the very first proposal went far beyond those instructions. It proposed to scrap the Articles of Confederation and write a totally new document upon which American government would be based.

At the center of this debate was the young Virginian, James Madison. He had come to Philadelphia with a new plan of government in mind. To give his ideas greater weight, Madison convinced the governor of Virginia, Edmund Randolph, to be the one to present his plan to the Convention. This Virginia Plan, as it became known, called for a more powerful central government than existed under the Articles of Confederation.

JAMES MADISON (1751-1836)

James Madison was born near Fredericksburg, Virginia, about 50 miles north of Richmond. He was the oldest of 12 children.

Although Madison was a frail and sickly child, he was a good student. It is said that after he entered the College of New Jersey (now Princeton University) at age 18, he studied so hard that he sometimes slept only five hours a night. As a result, Madison completed the college in just two years.

After college, Madison spent the next six months studying Hebrew, philosophy, and other subjects relating to his interest in religion. A weak speaking voice prevented him from becoming a minister.

Madison was elected to the first Virginia Assembly in 1776. He was elected to the Continental Congress in 1780 and was soon generally recognized as its ablest member. He returned to Virginia in 1783 to serve in the state legislature.

Although only 36 years old at the Constitutional Convention, Madison still became known as the Father of the Constitution.

Madison's plan called for power to be shared by three great branches of government:
- The legislative branch
- The executive branch
- The judicial branch

The legislative branch would make the laws. The executive branch would enforce the laws and carry out the business of running the government. The judicial branch would review the laws to ensure that they were in line with the Constitution.

In addition, the plan called for Congress to be a *bicameral* legislature.

That is, it would be made up of two houses, a House of Representatives and a Senate. Laws would have to be passed by both houses of Congress, but would no longer require a unanimous vote, as under the Articles of Confederation. Most importantly, the new government would be supreme over the states.

Under the Articles of Confederation, each state was represented equally with one vote. The Virginia Plan — Madison's — proposed that the number of representatives to Congress be determined by a state's population. This was known as *proportional representation*, or representation based upon population. Larger states like Virginia would be the big winners under this plan. The smaller states objected hotly. They were afraid they "would be swallowed up."

For a while, this dispute seemed to

James Madison

be without a solution. The delegates grew weary and argumentative. The stifling summer heat of Philadelphia didn't help. It was made worse by hours of debate in a closed room, with all windows and doors shut to preserve the secrecy of the deliberations. Finally, a committee headed by Benjamin Franklin was appointed to resolve the situation. Franklin was a good choice. He reminded the delegates that when a carpenter has to join two pieces of wood, he takes a little from both to form a joint. This was Franklin's gentle reminder that a solution was possible only if both sides gave a little.

Roger Sherman, who at age 66 was the only man to have signed all four great American documents – the Articles of Association in 1774, the Declaration of Independence in 1776, the Articles of Confederation in 1777, and later the U.S. Constitution – finally presented a compromise. The U.S. Congress would be made up of two houses – that is, it would be a bicameral legislature.

The number of members of the lower house, the House of Representatives, would be based on population, giving each state proportional representation. That gave the larger states what they wanted. The upper house, or Senate, would have two senators from each state. That gave small states the power to protect themselves.

Laws would have to pass both houses. That way, the interests of both the large and the small states would be assured, and the legislative branch would have an additional separation of powers.

After much debate, the Convention finally adopted this measure in what was later called the Great Compromise, a move which saved the Constitutional Convention from falling apart.

THE THREE-FIFTHS COMPROMISE

Slavery was also an issue which threatened to destroy the Convention. Southern states wanted their slaves to be counted in determining the number of seats in the House of Representatives, but they did not want to count them for purposes of determining how much tax the states owed to the new federal government. Northern states thought the slaves should be counted for purposes of taxation, but not for representation. As a compromise, the two sides agreed to count three-fifths (60%) of the slaves for the purposes of both taxation and representation.

Still another slavery issue came up. The southern plantation owners were concerned that since Congress was given the power to tax imported goods, the north might be able to stop the importation of slaves by imposing high taxes. Eventually the Convention agreed that, for 20 years, until 1808, Congress could not do anything to prohibit the slave trade.

The final Constitution referred to slaves as "other persons." While many delegates were very angry about this compromise, without it the Convention would have certainly failed to form a government.

OTHER ARGUMENTS

Another lengthy debate concerned the power of the executive branch of government. How much power should the President have? Should there be one President or three? Should he be elected by a vote of the people, or selected by Congress? Should the President serve for a set term or for life? Should the President command the army and navy? If the President thought a law was bad, could he veto it? Could Congress then overturn that veto anyway with a two-thirds majority? If the President acted illegally, could he be impeached and thrown out of office?

Jefferson wrote from France that he was very concerned that the Presidency might wind up as a term for life, perhaps even being passed from father to son. As he wrote to John Adams, "the Presidency seems a bad edition of a Polish King." But Adams disagreed. If someone were popular enough to be elected over and over, "so much the better, it appears to me."

WASHINGTON'S INFLUENCE

As the debate went on, Washington's influence loomed large. This was not because he said very much — Washington said little during the entire convention — but because he was just there, reminding the delegates by his imposing presence that they were in all likelihood designing the presidency for him. There was little doubt in anyone's mind that Washington would be the first President. The delegates had

The statue of George Washington in front of Independence Hall in Philadelphia

confidence in his wisdom. Washington had been described as "indeed in every sense of the word, a wise, a good, and a great man." That view was widely shared. Remembering that Washington had been a loyal general in the Revolution, the delegates decided that the President should be the commander in chief of the armed forces.

The delegates knew Washington would never abuse the powers of the Presidency himself. After all,

Washington had turned down an offer from some of his officers who wanted to make him King of America. What they were worried about was who would follow him into office in later years.

To deal with these concerns, the Constitution made the office of the President accountable to Congress. Though the people elected the President directly, if the President was found guilty of serious offenses by Congress, then Congress could remove him from office. This was part of the system of checks and balances that kept power spread out to the greatest extent possible while still retaining enough power in the central government to enable it to govern effectively.

To this day, the debate continues over how best to separate the powers of government to keep this nation free. Everyone agrees that if one person or one group gets too much power, then freedom can vanish very quickly. Some think the central government has too much power today. They realize that a stronger central government may have been necessary at first, but wish the founding fathers had somehow built in provisions to return more power to the states as time went on. There are others, however, who think the central government needs to be stronger. You can still hear this debate going on today, any time you listen to political news.

THE FINAL DOCUMENT

The Constitution that was eventually approved was basically the

Virginia Plan, modified to give the smaller states a larger share of power. The separation of powers is seen in the three branches of government — executive, legislative, and judicial. Each branch of government has its own power and responsibility. Checks and balances, on the other hand, give each branch some control over the others.

For example, here's how the three branches are involved in making a new law.

- Congress passes a bill,
- But it doesn't become a law unless the President signs it.
- If the President refuses to sign it, or vetoes it,
- Congress can still pass the law over the President's veto, if two-thirds of both houses of Congress pass it again. This is known as a veto override.

ONCE A LAW TAKES EFFECT

- The President is responsible for *enforcing* the law.
- The courts help *support* the President's enforcement responsibilities by interpreting the fine points of the laws.
- Congress *approves the money* necessary to enforce the law.
- The Supreme Court can review the law if it is challenged and decide whether it is *constitutional* or not.

Alexander Hamilton described the interaction of the branches in this way:

The Executive not only dispenses the honors, but holds the sword of the community. The Legislature not only commands the purse, but prescribes the rules by which the duties and rights of every citizen are to be regulated. The Judiciary, on the contrary, has no influence over either the sword or the purse ... and can take no active resolution whatever. It may truly be said to have neither force nor will, but merely judgment.

MISSING – A BILL OF RIGHTS

By late August 1787, with their work nearly completed, a few delegates still argued that the draft Constitution lacked something that most of the state constitutions had, a Bill of Rights. These men, led by George Mason from Virginia, argued that a Bill of Rights was needed to protect citizens against possible tyranny. They threatened to oppose the Constitution without such a bill.

Most of the delegates felt the draft plan provided enough protection from government excesses. Besides, they were tired of being away from their homes and families. Drafting, debating, and agreeing upon a Bill of Rights would take even more time. The Convention decided against a Bill of Rights.

THE PREAMBLE

Now the document was given to delegate Gouverneur Morris of Pennsylvania to be polished into final written form. Morris decided to rewrite the introduction to the Constitution, called the *Preamble*. The original Preamble still talked about the nation as being a collection of states. Morris knew that the intent of the new Constitution was towards a more united nation – to create one nation from a united people. His stirring 52-word preamble has been memorized by students ever since.

> We, the People of the United States, in order to form a more perfect union, establish justice, insure domestic tranquillity, provide for the common defense, promote the general welfare, and secure the blessings of liberty to ourselves and our posterity, do ordain and establish this Constitution for the United States of America.

FRANKLIN'S INFLUENCE

Finally, by the middle of September 1787, the final draft had been completed. The 42 delegates who remained at the Convention were anxious to finish their work and return home. Still, very few of them were happy with all of the document.

Benjamin Franklin rose to address the Convention to offer advice — advice which all Americans could benefit from if put to use in their day-to-day dealings. Young James Madison quickly took note of Franklin's words, so they are handed down to us just the way he spoke them. Franklin began:

> Mr. President. I confess that there are several parts of this Constitution which I do not at present approve, but I am not sure I shall never approve them. For, having lived long, I have experienced many instances of being obliged, by better information or fuller consideration, to change opinions, even on important subjects, which I once thought right but found to be otherwise. It is, therefore, that the older I grow, the more apt I am to doubt my own judgment and to pay more respect to the judgment of others....

Then Franklin urged the delegates to vote for the Constitution.

> On the whole, sir, I cannot help expressing a wish that every member of the Convention who may still have objections to it would with me, on this occasion, doubt a little of his own infallibility and ... put his name to this instrument.

As his fellow delegates were signing the document, Franklin studied a carved sun on the back of George Washington's chair. Finally, he remarked to those around him that all during the debates of the Convention, he had been unable to tell whether it was a rising sun or a setting sun. "But now," he said, "I have the happiness to know that it is a rising and not a setting sun."

Franklin, in his unique way, was predicting a bright future for the young nation under its new Constitution.

1788: THE APPROVAL PROCESS

Franklin's prophecy was, of course, dependent upon the approval of the new Constitution. Although most of the delegates had signed the Constitution, three did not: George Mason and Edmund Randolph from the all-important state of Virginia; and Elbridge Gerry of Massachusetts. These men returned home to work against approval.

The small state of Delaware won the honor of being the first state to approve – or ratify – the Constitution on December 7, 1787. Before the end of the year, New Jersey and Pennsylvania became the second and third states to ratify. Georgia and Connecticut ratified in January of 1788. In February 1788, Massachusetts, a state crucial to the general acceptance of the Constitution, ratified the document. But the margin of victory in Massachusetts was narrow. A change of only ten votes in the Massachusetts convention would have defeated ratification.

Next came Maryland, and then South Carolina. Many states ratified the Constitution with the reservation that a Bill of Rights must be added. In June of 1788, the debates over ratification of the new Constitution came up in both Virginia and New York. Throughout the states, powerful groups had formed to oppose ratification. Friends of the Constitution were known as the Federalists. Opponents of ratification were called the Anti-Federalists. Both sides promoted their causes in newspapers, in pamphlets, and in debates at their state conventions.

THE FEDERALIST PAPERS

In New York, the strong opposition to the Constitution stemmed primarily from the lack of a Bill of Rights and a fear that New York would be giving up far too much power to the central government. To try to sway public opinion in favor of the Constitution's ratification, three prominent men – Alexander Hamilton and John Jay of New York, and James Madison of Virginia – wrote a series of anonymous articles for a New York newspaper. Hamilton wrote most of the essays, and the most important ones too. In these articles, which became known as the *Federalist Papers*, they explained the provisions of the new Constitution and argued that it was far better than the old Articles of Confederation. Today, these arguments rank among the most brilliant political writings of all time.

Ratification of the Constitution was nearing an end. Eight states had already approved it – nine were needed for it to become the law of the land. Although mighty Massachusetts was one of these eight, its delegates had suggested that changes or amendments be added to the Constitution after it was ratified. New York, another key state, was on the fence about ratifying this new form of government without changes. And to the south, Virginia – the state with the greatest population in the new union – was also full of doubts and still had not voted to ratify. Just one more state was needed to change the whole country. It would be a close fight.

JUNE, 1788

Jed Warwick was elected as a delegate to vote on whether Virginia should ratify the Constitution. Like

John Jay, America's first Chief Justice of the Supreme Court.

many people in the established eastern part of the state, near the Atlantic coast, Jed wanted a more united government. Called a Federalist, he wanted the new nation to have stronger central leadership, so decisions could be made for the entire country.

George Washington was a Federalist, too. Jed remembered how difficult it had been to get the states to cooperate during the Revolution. If the states wanted to send troops, money, and supplies to the Continental Army, they did. If they didn't want to do so, there was nothing Washington could do to make them. From Mount Vernon, Washington had grumbled about the state of the nation under the Articles of Confederation. "Weak at home and disregarded abroad is our present condition, and contemptible enough it is."

Though Washington did not attend the state convention called to consider ratification of the new Constitution, everyone knew where he stood. Vote yes!

Jed, like others in Virginia, was not so sure. Many of the delegates opposed to a strong central government, called Anti-Federalists, came from the central and western parts of vast Virginia. At that time Virginia still included land today known as West Virginia and Kentucky. Even old Patrick Henry had spoken for the Anti-Federalist side when he had refused to take part in the Constitutional Convention in Philadelphia, complaining that he "smelt a rat."

Henry and others thought the Constitution still needed a Bill of Rights. Even Washington's old friend,

George Mason, refused to sign because citizens' basic freedoms were not defined or protected. What about guaranteed freedom of speech? Freedom of religion? The right of citizens to own guns to serve in the militia? Without these freedoms ensured by the new document, Mason feared the new nation was heading back toward "a monarchy or a corrupt, tyrannical aristocracy."

Writing from France, Jefferson agreed that, without such rights spelled out, the powers given to the President under the new Constitution might soon render him a king. Even if Washington himself might be trusted to be the first President, who would come after him?

Before heading off to the ratification meeting in Richmond, Jed Warwick talked it over with his old friend, John Crawford. John had lost his leg at the Battle of Guilford Courthouse and he owed his life to Jed's pulling him to safety. Since the war, the two had grown even closer. Both had struggled to re-settle their lives after the war. It had not been easy. They never had been fully paid for their military service, leaving their families in poverty. What good was some far-off new government for ordinary people like them?

Jed and John sat down in the Warwick's kitchen to mull things over. John lit his clay pipe with a few quick puffs. "I don't know," he murmured, pipe smoke curling up to the beamed ceiling. "I'm glad it's you going off to vote on this thing and not me. I wouldn't know what to do, myself. I've heard that there's no mention of the right to a trial by jury in this new Constitution."

Jed nodded his head, deep in thought. "That's true, but we do have that right now in Virginia. I hear most states do as well. I guess things like that will get worked out in the new government too." Jed's voice sounded uncertain. "But I can tell you this, there's a big group of delegates who have promised to add our rights on afterwards in what they call amendments to the Constitution. I wouldn't be going if I didn't believe that. After all, John, everybody knows that's what we fought the war over."

John looked less than convinced, knocking the end of his pipe against his hand over the brick fireplace. "But how do you know it won't be just like before? The only difference this time is it would be a bunch of rich people up north telling us what to do instead of a king. You know what George Mason called it, 'the tyranny of the aristocracy.' I don't trust those Yankees. What do they know about a couple of farmers like us down here in Virginia?"

"I trust them," Jed answered with more assurance. "I got to know lots of them trooping around this big old land during the war. Sure those Yankees talk funny – could barely understand a word they said sometimes. But those boys from Boston up in Massachusetts didn't like anybody telling them what to do more than you and I put together! Good men, too. I'd march again with them any day – real fighters. I hear General Washington's for this new Constitution. How are we going to get stronger for the next time around if we all don't band together a little tighter."

John looked down at the floor. He didn't have an answer. "Perhaps you're right, Jed," he finally said. Then as he looked out the window into the dark, he mumbled, "Maybe this country has to move on to something bigger. But a bigger what? All I know is that things aren't so bad in Virginia now. Don't go off and give away all our rights."

Jed nodded. "I won't, my friend. We fought too hard for them."

The next day, Jed left for the convention before dawn. All the famous men from around the state were there: James Monroe, John Marshall, the Lees, and others. Patrick Henry was there too. He was still as imposing as everyone had described, just a bit stooped over with age. Still, when he rose to speak, people listened. Those in favor of the Constitution were terrified that he alone could defeat it with one dramatic speech.

Jed had seen Henry and his old friend, George Mason, dressed in black, walking from the Swan Tavern to the meeting hall, obviously strong allies against ratification. Then, sitting across the room, was little James Madison – the main author of the Constitution – ready to take them on.

As the debate began, Madison defended his document in a weak voice. He was so short that Jed had trouble picking him out across the room. But when he stood, Jed could see his neat powdered ponytail hanging down below the collar of his beautiful dark-blue coat. And as the hours went on, Jed gained new respect for Madison. He ably fended off every objection to the new Constitution.

"What on earth could I have to say?" thought Jed to himself after listening to the debate of such learned men. He listened, along with the silent, steely-eyed frontiersmen who kept their pistols beneath their coats. They'd had to pass through Indian country to make the journey to Richmond.

Henry rose again to speak. "Where is the spirit of America gone?" he thundered. "Where is the genius of America fled?" The delegates sat in awe as torrents of eloquence flowed from Henry's lips. Even nature seemed to be in agreement as bolts of lightning shook the building outside from a raging thunderstorm. Who had changed things from "We the States" to this new "We the People?" Henry jabbed. Who were these upstarts who dared to speak for the people? Where were they leading this nation – to new chains of some all-powerful government? A few in the audience felt at their wrists as if the chains were already there. What was wrong with Virginia just the way it was, Henry challenged?

"Nothing," Jed thought to himself.

Another Anti-Federalist, William Grayson, rose to make fun of the Federalist fears over having no Constitution. Maryland and Pennsylvania were no doubt about to swoop down on Virginia just like wild barbarians in ancient times, he scoffed. South Carolina also was crawling up from the south "mounted on alligators, I presume, to destroy our cornfields and eat up our little children!"

174

The States began to ratify the Constitution because they felt sure that George Washington would become the first president. Washington was trusted by most citizens in both the North and South, and he was a proven leader. Here an artist depicts Washington's arrival in New York City for his inauguration as president.

Jed laughed along with the rest at the very idea. After the laughter died down, Grayson touched on more serious concerns. "We are yet too young to know what we are fit for," he worried. He thought this new government was too much too soon. The Anti-Federalists in the room nodded in agreement. Who could govern states as far away from each other as New Hampshire and Georgia? Over a thousand miles separated them.

Madison answered Grayson's charges. Occasionally glancing down into his hat to a few notes he had made to keep himself on track, he asked if people in New Hampshire and Georgia were really that narrow-minded? "Does not our own experience teach us that the people are better informed than they were a few years ago?"

Jed silently nodded yes, recalling the larger view of his own wonderful country he had gained during the war.

Surely such better understanding of each other can only grow under the Constitution, Madison pleaded. But Madison felt he was in the minority. His voice trailed off so that few could hear him.

But deep down, something began to stir in Jed. His respect for Madison was growing. He was not a commanding presence like General Washington, but

175

Jed could tell he was sincere, and Jed had probably seen more of the country than most of the delegates in that room.

Suddenly, Edmund Randolph, the handsome young Governor of Virginia rose to speak. He, like George Mason, had refused to sign the Constitution, even though he had worked on the original text in Philadelphia. But now, Randolph had changed his mind. He pointed out that eight states had already ratified the Constitution without Virginia, and now he felt it was too late to back out. Randolph suggested that Virginia ratify the Constitution and add the changes guaranteeing the freedoms about which everyone was so concerned afterward. That's what Massachusetts had done.

The idea seemed reasonable to Jed.

But then, Patrick Henry, Virginia's first governor, rose to his feet again, his voice full of mocking disbelief. "Something extraordinary must have operated so great a change in his opinions," he roared.

None too quietly, a nearby delegate murmured, "Bet General Washington got to him!"

Randolph was deeply hurt. His integrity had been questioned. He stood and looked Henry straight in the eye. "If our friendship must fall," Randolph boomed, "then let it go down to the devil never to rise again!"

The room grew silent. Everyone knew that Randolph was as loyal a Virginian as Henry or any other Anti-Federalist.

For three long weeks the angry debates continued. Randolph had almost been challenged to a duel because of his stand. Henry threatened to go home if the Constitution was passed before the guarantees of rights were added. Who was right? Jed still didn't know.

Picking up on Henry's threat to quit, Randolph finally put him on the defensive. Was Henry going home because he wanted Virginia to drop out? Jed definitely knew where he stood on that. He waited breathlessly for Henry to answer.

Henry sadly shook his head. To break up the confederation was too terrible for him to even think about.

The time had finally come to vote on the matter. Jed knew what he had to do. As each delegate's name was called in alphabetical order, each stood up to speak their mind. Opinions were clearly split down the middle – aye or nay – yes or no. Ten from Kentucky voted "nay," but four of them voted "aye." As the votes added up, tensions mounted. Cheers broke out after each vote was cast.

As the secretary reached the W's, Jed knew his time to vote had finally come. "Aye," he called out. The hall thundered in cheers. The Constitution – to be changed later – had been ratified in Virginia by a vote of 89 to 79. Jed left with the others to celebrate at the Swan Tavern. As he lifted his mug, he gave a little toast under his breath. "Here's to you and me, John. I just hope and pray I did the right thing."

Little did the delegates realize that New Hampshire had already put the Constitution over the top by voting yes *four days earlier, on June 21, 1788. New York ratified it a month later, on July 26. Although the American union was now on its way, North Carolina and Rhode Island refused to ratify the Constitution and take part in the new government until Congress agreed to add the statement of freedoms known as the Bill of Rights.*

Despite the compromises and the heated debates over ratification, the document that came out of the Pennsylvania State House in the summer of 1787 was a plan of government which has lasted longer than any other written constitution in human history. The United States Constitution has been modified only 27 times since then — or only 17 times if we don't count the 10 amendments comprising the Bill of Rights which were all adopted at one time in 1791. The ultimate tribute to those who authored our Constitution is that, since then, it has served as the model for the whole world as nations struggle to perfect their own forms of government.

Washington and his family experienced "the golden years" at Mount Vernon between the Revolutionary War and his two terms as president. Here you see Washington with Lafayette, Mrs. Washington, and her two grandchildren, Nelly and Washy.

President and Mrs. Washington held a number of social events in their New York and Philadelphia houses, and Washington was known as an excellent dancer. At left, the desk at Gunston Hall where George Mason penned so many letters arguing for stronger states' rights. Political differences between Washington and Mason caused their friendship to sour in the later years of their lives.

Chapter 18

The First Days of the Constitutional Republic

GEORGE WASHINGTON ELECTED PRESIDENT

The first election for President of the United States took place early in 1789. Under our Constitution, when we vote for President and Vice President, we actually are voting for electors who have promised to vote for a particular candidate. That system was set up because when the Constitution was

written there were no telephones or other modern means of communications, and travel was hard and slow. It is one of the most cumbersome features of the Constitution, but even to this day, that's the way we elect a President.

George Washington, now known as "the father of his country," was unanimously elected as the first President of the new nation. John

Adams was elected as its first Vice-President. They, along with the new Congressmen and Senators, traveled to the temporary capital in New York City and were sworn in on the first Inaugural Day, April 30, 1789. Congress later made Philadelphia the new, though still temporary, capital of the nation.

Soon thereafter, in 1790, Benjamin Franklin died. As Americans mourned the passing of a comforting father figure of the past, they nervously looked toward a new beginning.

PROBLEMS OF THE NEW GOVERNMENT

Enormous problems confronted Washington. He had to be very careful in everything he did because he knew that each decision he made was defin-

General Henry Knox, President George Washington's first Secretary of War.

ing the relationship between the different branches of government. In other words, every decision set a precedent. Precedents are actions which people in the future look back on to follow as examples. "I walk on untrodden ground," Washington wrote a friend. "There is scarcely any part of my conduct which may not hereafter be drawn into precedent."

In addition, the new government had serious national and international problems. The economy was in chaos. Many Americans were distrustful of the new government and its intentions. On the western frontier, Indian tribes were being encouraged by the British and the Spanish to attack American settlers. The British still held on to forts on the frontier despite their promise to abandon them at the end of the Revolution. On the sea, pirates raided American ships in the Mediterranean and held United States citizens hostage, asking for ransom to release them or else keeping them in slavery.

APPOINTING THE FIRST CABINET

The first order of business, however, was to set up the executive and the judicial branches of government. Washington needed help to run the government, so Congress quickly voted to establish three departments within the executive branch: the Departments of War, State, and the Treasury. Washington picked men he knew well and trusted to head up these departments. These men would be Washington's closest advisors – his Cabinet. He selected Henry Knox, his former chief of artillery, to run the War Department. He chose Thomas Jefferson to head up the State Department. He named Alexander Hamilton as the first Secretary of Treasury. Finally, Washington asked Edmund Randolph of Virginia to be the nation's first Attorney General, the top legal officer.

It wasn't long, however, before the other great men working in the new government divided into two camps: the "Federalists" formed around Hamilton; and the opposing side (no longer called Anti-Federalists, but Republicans) formed around Jefferson. These factions made Washington's work much more difficult.

THE JUDICIARY

Congress had to create a new federal court system to administer the laws. While the Constitution called for a Supreme Court to be the highest court in the land, it left the job of deciding its size to Congress. Appointments to the new court would be made by the President and approved by the Senate. Washington appointed John Jay to be the Chief Justice, along with five Associate Justices. Congress also created a district court system to hear most federal cases.

THE BILL OF RIGHTS

Now Congress turned its attention to the Bill of Rights. Several states had passed the Constitution only with the understanding that the first Congress must add a Bill of Rights to the document in the form of amendments.

James Madison, now a Congressman from Virginia, originally had thought a Bill of Rights was not necessary. But after the refusal of Patrick Henry to join the new government, and considering that North Carolina and Rhode Island had still not ratified the Constitution, Madison changed his mind. He drafted a Bill of Rights for Congress. It was in the form of ten amendments to the Constitution.

These first ten amendments became part of the Constitution in 1791. They ensure the following freedoms:

Amendment 1: Freedom of religion, speech, press, assembly and petition.

Amendment 2: Right to keep and bear arms.

Amendment 3: Quartering of troops in private houses without permission of the owner is prohibited.

Amendment 4: Protection against unreasonable searches and seizures.

Amendment 5: Spells out the rights of those accused of crimes, such as the right to have the charges against the accused

Alexander Hamilton, President George Washington's first Secretary of the Treasury

heard by a grand jury, protection against being tried twice for the same crime, and protection against having to testify against yourself.

Amendment 6: Spells out the right to a speedy and public trial.

Amendment 7: The right to have civil cases heard by a jury.

Amendment 8: Protection against excessive bail, excessive fines, and cruel and unusual punishment.

Amendment 9: Says that those powers not given by the Constitution to some arm of government are retained by the people.

Amendment 10: Says that those powers not given by the Constitution to the federal government are retained by the states or by the people.

Once the states ratified the Bill of Rights, most people who had previously opposed the Constitution accepted it — even Patrick Henry. North Carolina and Rhode Island soon joined the United States.

HAMILTON VERSUS JEFFERSON

Once the government was beginning to function, and once the Bill of Rights question had been settled, Washington turned his attention to the two major problems facing him: the economy and protecting the nation in a hostile world. Congress asked Alexander Hamilton, the new Secretary of the Treasury, for ideas on the economy. Thomas Jefferson, as Secretary of State, was the one to advise Washington on foreign affairs. However, each of these men had ideas about the right thing to do regarding the other's area of responsibility, and as time went on, Hamilton and Jefferson were constantly feuding.

Hamilton found much to admire in Great Britain. After all, Great Britain was still the most powerful country in the world. He hoped that America would one day become as wealthy and powerful. For that reason, he believed the federal government should be as strong as possible.

Hamilton believed that the best way to create national wealth and power was to let businessmen lead the nation. If their economic interests were protected, they would naturally create a huge economic engine in the United States, just as they had done in Great Britain.

Jefferson had a different view of America's future. He believed that America already had great wealth in its land and that the nation's future economic prosperity lay not in industry, but in agriculture. This did not mean that Jefferson was against manufacturing. But he felt it was agriculture where America had a great advantage over Europe. He thought it would be easier for Americans to trade food for whatever manufactured goods the nation needed. After all, most of the people still lived in the country, not in towns.

Eventually, these differences led to the development of the country's first political parties. Jefferson led the Democratic-Republicans, and Hamilton led the Federalists.

Washington pleaded with both Hamilton and Jefferson to maintain the unity of the administration, but this was impossible. "How unfortunate," Washington told Jefferson, "that internal dissensions should be harrowing and tearing our vitals." Unless their bickering stopped, "in my opinion the fairest prospect of happiness and prosperity that ever was presented to man will be lost – perhaps forever!"

WASHINGTON'S VISION FOR AMERICA

Despite the feuding between Hamilton and Jefferson, Washington was still very much in control. The most important thing to the new President was unity.

Washington can truly be called a nation builder because his primary goal was to merge all 13 states and the American people into one great nation. Everything else was secondary, and in the space of the eight years of his administration he largely brought this about. Considering how chaotic the nation had been at the start of his presidency, this was a remarkable achievement.

WAR DEBTS

One of the first disagreements between Hamilton and Jefferson was over the issue of debts created during the Revolutionary War. The Continental Congress and the various states had all borrowed money to support the war. Also, they owed back pay to some of the soldiers who fought in the war.

The United States government and the separate states owed a combined war debt of more than $80,000,000, a staggering sum for those days. About $12,000,000 of this was owed to France, the Netherlands, and Spain. Everyone agreed that it should be paid.

The domestic debt (the internal debt) was another matter. Hamilton believed that these debts had to be paid off to show the world that the United States intended to keep its financial promises. Hamilton also wanted the new federal government to pay off any remaining state debts as well. These debts, he argued, had been caused by participation in the war effort, so they should be paid by the federal government. This would also show that the federal government had control over the national economy.

But Hamilton's proposal met with much criticism. Some people thought it would be unfair as well as expensive to pay off all the debts.

Eventually, however, a compromise was struck. Jefferson and Madison would let the federal government pay the internal debts if the future national capital was moved southward to the Potomac River in northern Virginia. This would boost the economy and prestige of the area.

THE FRENCH REVOLUTION

A revolution broke out in France in 1789, the year Washington took office as President. The French Revolution was quite different from the American Revolution. Americans didn't throw out English law; they based their government upon it and moved quickly to establish a stable government.

Although the success of the American Revolution gave hope to some Frenchmen that they too could enjoy a life free from rule by a King or a small group of powerful men, the French Revolution had quite a different ending. The groups who wanted a republi-can government in France did not work well together and ruling parties changed hands several times during a violent period at the end of the century.

In France, barbarism ruled the streets. Mass executions were common. So many were killed that blood actually ran in the streets of Paris. The revolutionary government overthrew King Louis XVI, imprisoned him and his wife, Marie Antoinette, and eventually cut off their heads.

Jefferson was the American minister to France when the revolution broke out. Alarmed at what he saw in the initial stages of the French Revolution, he wrote home to a friend:

> The cutting off of heads is so *a la mode* [French for in style] that one is apt to feel in the morning whether their own is on their shoulders.

As the French revolution grew increasingly bloody, other Americans became disgusted with it. After the executions of Louis XVI and his wife, most of Europe turned against France as well.

As a result, war broke out in 1793 pitting France against most of the European powers, including Great Britain. President Washington tried to steer a neutral course between the warring countries. This, however, became increasingly difficult as people in the United States took sides.

Hamilton supported the British side. Jefferson argued that America should support its former ally, France, who had done so much to help America in her fight for freedom. As the controversy deepened, Hamiltonian's Federalists and Jefferson's Democratic-Republicans saw each other as dangerous to the future of the nation. The Federalists considered the French revolutionaries as little better than murderers. Jefferson's followers imagined that the Federalists were hatching dark plans to return America to the British Empire. This was a most crucial period in our history.

EDMOND GENÊT

In April 1793, the revolutionary government in France appointed Edmond Genêt as its minister to the United States. At that time, the French had seized American ships carrying goods to Great Britain, and the British had seized other American ships carrying goods to France.

Genêt wanted privately owned American ships to attack British ships on behalf of the French government. These privateers would then get to keep the captured ships and the cargo.

Many Americans welcomed Genêt and called upon Washington to come to France's aid. But the President wanted America to stay out of any war. On April 22, 1793, he issued a Proclamation of Neutrality which forbade American citizens to take part in any hostilities.

The French trouble-maker tried to go over Washington's head and whip up the American people to oppose their President. This was a tremendous embarrassment to Jefferson and the Republicans. Perhaps the French revolutionaries were not as well-intentioned as they had thought.

Washington finally exploded over the whole matter after a newspaper suggested that Washington should have his head cut off just like the French monarch. Jefferson recorded the dramatic moment:

> The President was much inflamed, got into one of those passions when he cannot command himself, ran on [about] the personal abuse which had been bestowed upon him, defied any man on earth to produce one single act of his since he had been in government which was not done on the purest motives ... [and that] by God he had rather be in his grave than in his present situation. That he would rather be on his farm than to be made emperor of the world and yet that they were charging him with wanting to be a king.

However, Washington held the loyalty of the American people. They did not follow Genêt, who fell out of favor both in the United States and France. In fact, he discovered that if he returned to his own country he would likely be beheaded. Washington generously allowed him to stay in the United States, thereby sparing his life. He married, became an American citizen, and lived here the rest of his life.

JAY'S TREATY

On the high seas, and especially in Caribbean ports, British ships began capturing American ships and forcing American sailors to work for the British Navy. Despite Washington's Proclamation of Neutrality, this made war with Britain seem nearly certain.

The President knew that another war with Great Britain would be a disaster, for the United States had almost no army. He sent John Jay – the Chief Justice of the Supreme Court – to London to try to resolve the dispute.

Jay returned with a treaty. It said that British troops would withdraw from American forts in the west. But Britain refused to pay compensation for the captured American ships until the Americans paid British merchants and Loyalists for their property which was seized during the American Revolution.

Jay's Treaty, as it was called, was seen at first by some of the followers of Jefferson as a sellout to Great Britain. Angry mobs threw stones at Hamilton and burned a figure of Jay. They did not realize that the treaty had accomplished its main goal – keeping America out of a war with Great Britain.

In the end, Washington used his enduring influence to win approval of Jay's Treaty in the Senate. The President knew that Jay had won all the concessions that the United States could reasonably expect to win from the most powerful country on earth. For now, it was more important for the new nation concentrate on problems at home.

OPENING THE FRONTIER

Washington's attention turned to opening the western frontier. For 20 years the Indians, given weapons and supplies by the British and the Spanish, had raided American towns and slowed settlement of the lands along the Ohio River. Washington was determined to put a stop to it.

The American army had suffered defeats at the hands of Indian tribes led by a warrior chief named Little Turtle. In the summer of 1794, Washington sent a veteran of the American Revolution, General "Mad Anthony" Wayne, with an army of 2,000 troops to go after Little Turtle.

General Wayne met Little Turtle's forces near where the Maumee River empties into Lake Erie, close to present day Toledo, Ohio. The Indians decided to fight where some years earlier a tornado had torn a two-mile long swath of twisted trees. They hid among these blown-down trees, thinking they would be an impregnable fortress. But Wayne's force included well trained regulars, full-time soldiers who were prepared for battle. On August 20, Wayne struck hard and fast, routing the Indians in about an hour. The victory became known as the Battle of the Fallen Timbers.

A year later, Wayne signed a peace treaty with the tribes in which they formally gave the territory north of the Ohio River to the United States. The British withdrew into Canada.

Around the same time, the United States negotiated a favorable treaty with the Spanish which opened the Mississippi River and New Orleans to U.S. trade. The treaty also won assurances from Spanish officials that they would not encourage Indian attacks against U.S. settlements.

THE WHISKEY REBELLION

Washington had to face another challenge to the federal government that year in western Pennsylvania. Congress had placed a tax on whiskey. Whiskey was the most important source of cash for many farmers who lived on the frontier. In 1794, a revolt developed in western Pennsylvania against paying the tax. Farmers refused to pay, and threatened the tax collectors with harm if they tried to enforce the law.

Washington saw the revolt as a direct challenge to the federal government. He personally led an army of about 15,000 men west to restore order. Not surprisingly, when the army arrived near Pittsburgh, few "Whiskey Rebels" were found. But the power of the federal government had been demonstrated.

WASHINGTON REFUSES A THIRD TERM

By 1796, Washington had created a solid government for the new republic. But he was weary; the political wrangling had taken its toll on him.

Had he wanted to seek a third term, there is no doubt he would have been re-elected, but he longed to return to his beloved Mount Vernon to live out his years as a farmer. He was 64 years old

General Anthony Wayne

and tired of political life. Besides, he was committed to a government where power changed hands frequently and peacefully, so he did not want to continue in office too long. This peaceful transfer of power may well have been his greatest achievement. We see it repeated every four years when we elect, then inaugurate a new president.

At the time, America was the first nation in modern history to try an elected form of democratic government, known as a constitutional republic. The rules by which the government operated were set up in the Constitution, and the people elected their representatives. By stepping down after two terms, Washington proved that a person of character can avoid being corrupted by power.

It is also important to realize that,

The President and other dignitaries gather to see the first American coins created by the new Bureau of Engraving. Since that time, George Washington's image has appeared on many coins and medals, including the quarters and dollar bills we still use today.

by this time, Washington had achieved all his major goals. He had created a united nation which would endure. He had successfully established the role of the federal government. He had brought peace to the frontier, kept America out of European wars, and he had established the nation's capital. As he'd hoped, the nation was growing into a union rather than a coalition of separate states. Therefore, he decided not to run for reelection in 1796. His decision set another precedent – that Presidents should not serve more than two terms. This precedent was broken only by President Franklin Roosevelt,

who served three full terms and part of a fourth before dying in office during World War II.

WASHINGTON'S FAREWELL ADDRESS

As Washington prepared to leave office, he was still troubled by the sharp division between the Hamiltonians and the Jeffersonians. He was also troubled that, after he was gone, others with less experience might be tempted to be drawn into the endless conflicts among the European nations.

As one of his last public acts, in late 1796, Washington delivered a Farewell Address to Congress. In it, he urged all Americans to remain devoted to the American union. He also counselled them to avoid political parties and "permanent alliances" with "any portion of the foreign world." Washington believed that foreign alliances would tie the hands of the nation and prevent the government from acting in its own best interests.

THE ELECTION OF 1796

The election of 1796 was the first in our history where there was a real contest. The Jeffersonians obviously favored Thomas Jefferson to succeed Washington as President. The Federalists favored John Adams, Washington's Vice-President for the last eight years.

Alexander Hamilton, however, did not like Adams. He secretly worked against him on behalf of another man, but without success. When the votes in the Electoral College were counted, Adams had 71, Jefferson had 68, and Hamilton's candidate had only 59. At that time, the Constitution stated that the candidate with the most votes would become the President and the one with the second-most votes would become the Vice-President. Adams thus became President and Jefferson Vice-President, even though they were from opposite political parties.

PEACEFUL TRANSFER OF POWER

On inauguration day, March 4, 1797, Washington, Adams, and Jefferson entered Congress Hall in Philadelphia – then the nation's capital. There, in the chamber used by the House of Representatives, and in the presence of Congress, John Adams took the oath of office as the new President of the United States.

Afterward, as they got ready to leave, Adams stepped aside at the door to allow Washington to go through first. But Washington was well aware of the historic significance of the moment. He stopped and asked Adams to leave first. After all, Adams was now President of the United States and George Washington was again just a private citizen. Adams led, followed by Jefferson, and Washington went last.

This was the first time in human political history that power was transferred between two common citizens without the death or violent overthrow of the person losing power. The Constitution had passed its first crucial test primarily because of George Washington's commitment to it and to the spirit of the American Revolution.

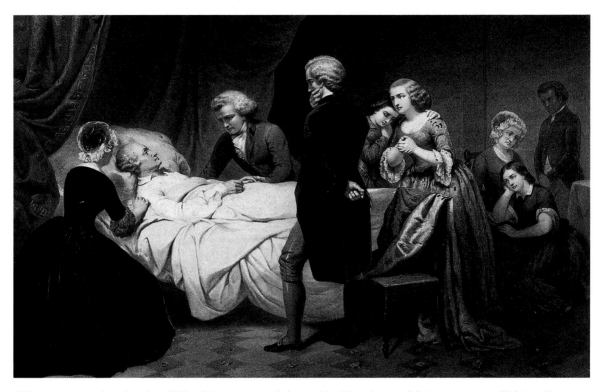

The scene at the death of Washington, with his wife Martha and his secretary Tobias Lear at his side. At left, the greenhouse structure at Mount Vernon, where growing exotic plants was one of Washington's favorite pastimes during his brief retirement.

Chapter 19

Freedom Isn't Free

After the inauguration of John Adams as the second President, George Washington, at age 65, finally returned home to his beloved Mount Vernon. Almost every day visitors came to see him. As he wrote later that year on July 31, 1797:

> Unless someone pops in unexpectedly – Mrs. Washington and myself will do what has not been done within the last twenty years by us – that is to set down to dinner by ourselves.

Managing the more than 8,000 acres which made up his Mount Vernon estate took much of Washington's time. He also made frequent trips to the new city of Washington, D.C., to watch the construction of the nation's new capitol.

During his last year of life, Washington was saddened by the deaths of friends and relatives. His old friend, Patrick Henry, died on June 6, 1799. Henry and Washington had a long and close friendship in Virginia politics. When Henry was asked who the greatest man in the Continental Congress was, he replied:

> If you speak of solid information and sound judgment, Colonel Washington is, unquestionably, the greatest man on the floor.

On December 12, 1799, Washington wrote his last letter about America. It was to Alexander Hamilton. He suggested the nation needed to establish a national military academy. That institution would become West Point.

WASHINGTON'S DEATH

After finishing the letter, Washington went for his daily horseback ride. The day was cold, with a mixture of snow and sleet falling. Washington returned after and ate dinner without changing his damp clothes. The next morning he awoke with a sore throat. He paid no attention to it, however, and went out to mark some trees for removal, despite the fact that it was snowing outside and was only 30 degrees.

When he came back inside, his secretary, Tobias Lear, remarked that he had gotten wet. Lear later wrote, "He said no, his great coat had kept him dry, but his neck appeared to be wet and the snow was hanging upon his hair." On retiring, Lear advised Washington to doctor his throat. He responded as he usually did concerning illnesses, "Let it go as it came."

That night his throat became very sore. He could barely speak when he awakened Martha between 2 and 3 a.m. But he wouldn't allow Martha to get up in the cold to summon a doctor until morning. One doctor arrived and said his illness was "inflammatory quinsy." Some modern doctors believe it was a bacterial infection of the throat. Back then, before antibiotics had been invented, there was no cure.

Later that afternoon, December 14, two other doctors arrived, but their only remedy was one popular at the time – they bled Washington, which was about the very worst thing they could have done to him. That night, about 10 o'clock, he instructed his secretary on the manner in which he wished to be buried. "Do you understand me?" Washington asked Lear. "Yes, sir," he replied sadly. Washington said, "'Tis well." Then he felt his own pulse and died quietly.

"Is he gone?" asked his wife, Martha. Lear could not speak while he held Washington's lifeless hand to his chest. "'Tis well," Martha said, as if alone in the room. "I shall soon follow him," and she did so a few years later. Both are buried at Mount Vernon, one of America's most popular shrines, visited by millions of people who want to learn about the "Father of His Country."

The nation mourned the death of George Washington. On December 18, 1799, he was given a grand funeral. John Marshall, then a Congressman, and later America's fourth Chief Justice of the Supreme Court, lamented the death of Washington:

> The hero, the sage, the patriot of America, the man on whom in times of danger every eye was turned and all hopes were placed, lives now only in his own great actions, and in the hearts of an affectionate and afflicted people.

Washington's fellow Virginian, Henry "Light Horse Harry" Lee, told a joint session of Congress that Washington was:

> ...the most illustrious and most beloved personage this country has ever produced.... First in war, first in peace, and first in the hearts of his countrymen, he was second to none in the humble and endearing scenes of private life....

For months after that, thousands of people wore mourning clothes.

No other American has been honored more than Washington. The nation's capital, Washington, D.C., is named for him. In the center of the city, the gigantic Washington Monument rises far above every other building.

These honors are as much a tribute to Washington's character as to the fact that he was the leader of the Revolution and the nation's first president. What is character? It is your habits, your behavior, your moral reputation. For example, George Washington was hum-ble. He was not arrogant. He accepted honors only with reluctance. That wasn't natural to him. It was a virtue he learned through practice. In other words, character isn't what you are born with and it is displayed by your behavior.

Remember the Rules of Civility Washington copied as a boy in school? Practicing modesty was one of those rules. Another was to treat everyone with courtesy, dignity, and politeness, and never arrogance. Washington practiced these rules all his life. That's what built his character – a character everyone he knew came to admire. As Washington's first biographer, Parson

Washington's desk at Mount Vernon.

The Tomb of George Washington at Mount Vernon is visited by almost a million people each year, and on every George Washington's Birthday, the sitting president sends a special wreath to honor "The Father of His Country."

Weems, put it, "no wonder every body honored him who honored every body."

In his eulogy, Gouverneur Morris noted that Washington's first victory was the victory of his character over his hot passions. "With them was his first contest, and his first victory was over himself."

A quarter century after the death of Washington, the French writer Chateaubriand wrote of him:

> The deeds of Washington were wrapped in silence; he was slow to act; it might be said that he felt himself entrusted with the liberty of the future and was afraid of placing it in jeopardy. This hero of unprecedented kind did not carry the burden of his own destiny, but the destiny of his own country; he could not risk that which did not belong to him; but from that deep humility what a light was to burst forth! Search the forests through which flashed the sword of Washington: what will be found? Tombs? No; a world. For a monument on the field of battle, Washington erected the United States.

JEFFERSON'S ELECTION

The year after Washington's death, in 1800, Thomas Jefferson was elected president over John Adams, the second President of the United States. President Adams was so upset about having to turn the Presidency over to his political enemy that he quietly left the capitol – by then in Washington, D.C. – the day before Jefferson was sworn into power. Adams did not want to witness the inauguration of a man he felt was a weak choice for such an important job.

This may seem like poor statesmanship, but obviously Adams felt very deeply about the direction of the nation. What is very significant is that Adams followed Washington's precedent and turned over the reins of power of the executive branch of government peacefully. Just as the election of 1796 was the first peaceful transfer of power, the election of 1800 has been called the Peaceful Revolution of 1800. It was the first peaceful transfer of power between political opponents from different parties.

This shows the respect these men gave to the Constitution, only a few years after its implementation. It also illustrates the success Americans had achieved in creating a society where men were free to attain their goals within a framework of laws. America was truly a government of laws and not of men.

FRIENDS AGAIN

Several years later, Jefferson and Adams became friends again, as they had been during those heady days of the Revolution. From 1812 to 1826, they carried on an amazing correspondence between their homes in Massachusetts and Virginia. They discussed and argued about all kinds of things, as friends do. But although they continued to disagree on some political matters, they came to understand the importance of the system they had helped create, one where competing political ideas and philosophies were not only tolerated, but encouraged.

THE REMARKABLE DEATHS OF ADAMS AND JEFFERSON

From the accounts of friends and relatives, we know that both Adams and Jefferson badly wanted to live until the 50th anniversary of the Declaration of Independence. Both men had grown weak from old age as the day approached in 1826. On the afternoon of July 4, 1826, the day of the 50th anniversary of the Declaration of Independence, in one of history's most incredible coincidences, both John Adams and Thomas Jefferson died. Adams' last words were "Thomas Jefferson still survives." What Adams did not know was that Jefferson had died only a few hours earlier, just before 1:00 p.m., on the 50th anniversary of the document he had written.

OUR RESPONSIBILITY

Fortunately, the Constitution they had all worked so hard to bring into being lives on – a shining example of humanity's triumph over its barbaric roots. These men had devoted their lives to see this goal achieved. Many other Americans, both men and women, have given their lives since then to preserve America's freedom. We know that their sacrifice was not in vain whenever we think about how blessed we are to live in the United States of America.

The importance of their sacrifices cannot be overrated. The best way we can honor all of them is by being sure we understand what the Founding Fathers did during that long-ago Revolutionary period, and why they did it.

But that's not the end of our responsibilities. We also have the responsibility of passing on our knowledge of the Founding Fathers and their accomplishments to those who come after us. That's why we study history. Most important of all, we need to use the opportunities they gave us; to participate in the process of our government, to vote, and to play an active role in the political and civic life of our communities.

Remember, freedom isn't free. It's our responsibility.

Glossary

Adams, John. Key leader in the revolutionary movement for independence; served the country as vice-president and as its second president.

Albany Plan of Union. Benjamin Franklin's plan for union of the colonies, proposed at a meeting in Albany, New York in 1754.

Anglican Church. The official church of Britain and the American colonies. It was supported by taxes collected by the government.

Anti-Federalist. Opposed to the Constitution during the ratification debates.

Arnold, Benedict. American officer who became a traitor and joined the British army.

Articles of Confederation. Plan of Government voted in November 1777 that enabled the states to cooperate during the Revolution.

Bicameral legislature. Form of American government consisting of a Senate and a House of Representatives.

Bill of Rights. First ten amendments to the U.S. Constitution, passed in 1791, that guaranteed specific personal liberties to American citizens.

Boston Massacre. On March 5, 1770, five Boston citizens were killed by British soldiers.

Boston Tea Party. On December 16, 1773, colonists disguised as Indians boarded ships in Boston harbor and dumped tea overboard as a protest over the Tea Act of 1773.

Braddock, Edward. British general who was defeated at Fort Duquesne during the French and Indian War.

British Empire. The nations and colonies under authority of the British King.

Bunker Hill, Battle of. On June 16, 1775, the British attacked a fortified position (on Breed's Hill) held by the Massachusetts Militia and colonists.

Cabinet. A group of officials chosen by the president to advise him on public policy.

Colonial scrip. Paper money issued by the British colonial governments in America.

Committees of Correspondence. Starting in 1772, groups of patriots who exchanged news about problems with the British.

Concord, Battle of. On April 19, 1775, one of the first major battles of the Revolution.

Constitutional Convention. Meeting in Philadelphia in 1787 of delegates from 11 colonies, during which the U.S. Constitution was drafted.

Constitution. Written document that explains how a country or state is to be governed.

Continental Army. Official name of colonists' army during Revolutionary War.

Cowpens, Battle of. British defeated at this battle in January 1781.

The Crisis. Pamphlet written by Thomas Paine in favor of independence for colonies.

Cornwallis, Charles. British general who surrendered at the Battle of Yorktown, thereby ending the Revolutionary War in 1781.

Currency Act of 1764. British law that prohibited the issue of scrip in the colonies.

Declaration of Independence. Act of Continental Congress of July 4, 1776, declaring that the British colonies in North America no longer belonged to the British Empire.

Delegate. Represents a group of people in a political meeting.

Democrat-Republican. Early political party that favored the rights of states.

Dunmore, Lord. British Governor of Virginia.

196

Fallen Timbers, Battle of. August 20, 1794, victory of General Wayne over Indian forces, opening the Ohio area to settlement.

Farewell Address. George Washington's final statement as president.

Federalist. Supported a Constitution during ratification debates. Also an early political party that favored a strong central government.

Federalist Papers. Series of essays written in support of a Constitution.

Fort Duquesne. Strategic location during the French and Indian War, near present-day Pittsburgh.

Fort Necessity. Defended by George Washington, this small fort in western Pennsylvania was captured by the French during the French and Indian War.

France. An important American ally during the Revolutionary War.

Franklin, Benjamin. American statesman who wisely advised the leaders of the Revolution in the formation and policy of the nation's new government.

French and Indian War. War fought between the British and the French and Indians for control of land for colonization and trade.

French Revolution. Overthrow of monarchy by French citizens in 1789.

Garrison. A small unit of soldiers taking up a defensive position to hold a town or fort.

George, III, King. Ruler of the British empire during the Revolutionary War.

Great Compromise. Agreement between representatives of small and large states at the Constitutional Convention, creating a House of Representatives and the Senate.

Green Mountain Boys. Soldiers from the Green Mountains of Vermont that helped the American forces capture Fort Ticonderoga.

Hays, Mary "Molly Pitcher." Female patriot who bravely carried water to thirsty soldiers during the Battle at Monmouth Courthouse.

Henry, Patrick. Virginia statesman whose fiery speeches motivated the patriots' fight for independence.

Hessians. German soldiers hired by the British to help fight the Continental Army.

House of Burgesses. A representative form of government in colonial Virginia.

Independence Hall. First called the Pennsylvania State House, this building was the site of important meetings, such as the Continental Congress and Constitutional Convention.

Infantry. A foot soldier who fights with musket and bayonet.

Intolerable Acts. British law re-authorizing the quartering of troops.

Jay's Treaty. Treaty with Britain negotiated by John Jay in 1793.

Jefferson, Thomas. Author of the Declaration of Independence; first Secretary of State; third president of the United States.

King Mountain, Battle of. In October 1780, it was the first British defeat in the south.

Lexington, Battle of. On April 19, 1775, it was the first battle of the Revolution.

Loyalists. Colonists who remained loyal to Great Britain.

Militia. Troops comprised of residents of a state to defend its boundaries.

Minutemen. Members of the colonists' militia who were trained to organize immediately.

Monmouth, Battle of. Continental Army victory in New Jersey in June 1778

Mount Vernon. George Washington's home on the banks of the Potomac River in Virginia.

New England Primer. A useful textbook for students in early America.

Newburgh Conspiracy. Threatened mutiny by Continental Army officers to demand back pay. Stopped by Washington.

Parliament. Legislative body of the British government.

Patriots. Colonists who favored breaking ties with Great Britain.

Philadelphia. Site of important meetings before and during the Revolutionary War; site of the capital of the United States, 1790-1800.

Preamble. The introduction to the Constitution.

Proclamation of 1763. A British edict ordering settlers to withdraw to the east of the Appalachians.

Proclamation of Neutrality. Statement by President George Washington on April 22, 1793, maintaining neutrality in the war between Britain and France.

Quartering Act. Forced colonists to provide room and board for British soldiers.

Ratification. The approval process of the Constitution, voted on by individual states.

Redcoats. The name that colonists gave to the British soldiers who wore red coats.

Revere, Paul. Massachusetts patriot who alerted citizens that British "redcoats" were approaching Lexington and Concord.

Revolutionary War. War for independence between the colonies and Britain, 1775-1783.

Rochambeau, Comte de. Leader of the French forces at the British surrender at the Battle of Yorktown.

Rules of Civility. Book of rules of etiquette and proper behavior copied by George Washington as a youth.

Saratoga, Battle of. Continental Army victory at Saratoga, New York on Oct. 17, 1777.

Shays' Rebellion. Uprising of farmers in Massachusetts, protesting seizure of farms.

"Sons of Liberty". Colonial societies that resisted British laws in the colonies.

Stamp Act of 1765. Required government tax stamp on all official papers.

Steuben, Baron von. Prussian officer brought to America to train the Continental Army with great efficiency.

Sugar Act of 1764. Tax on molasses, sugar and other imports into the British colonies.

Tories. American loyalists to the British crown who opposed American independence.

Townshend Acts. Acts passed in 1767 taxing goods that were imported into the colonies.

Treaty of Paris. Peace treaty between Britain, Spain and France ending the French and Indian War.

Valley Forge. Winter encampment of the Continental Army, 1777-1778.

Virginia Plan. Plan for a strong national government, proposed by Virginia delegates to the Constitutional Convention.

Washington, George. Commander in Chief of the Continental Army. Became first president of the United States. Made his home at Mount Vernon, Virginia.

Whiskey Rebellion. Uprising of western Pennsylvania farmers in 1794 against taxes on whiskey.

Writs of Assistance. Law allowing British officials to search for smuggled goods in colonists' homes and businesses.

Yankee. Term describing Continental soldiers and residents of New England

Yorktown, Battle of. Battle in Virginia ending the Revolutionary War in 1781.

Index

Illustrations are *italicized*

List of Illustrations